Gateway to Hope

Maria Boulding is a contemplative nun at Stanbrook Abbey in England. She is the author of *Prayer: Our Journey Home*, *The Coming of God*, and also played an important role in the writing of *Consider Your Call*.

The book which she edited, *A Touch of God*, is available from St. Bede's.

Gateway to Hope

An Exploration of Failure

MARIA BOULDING

ST. BEDE'S PUBLICATIONS
Petersham, Massachusetts

First published in 1985 by Fount Paperbacks, London
Copyright © 1985 by Maria Boulding
This edition is published by arrangement with
Edward England Books, Crowborough, East Sussex
All Rights Reserved
PRINTED IN THE UNITED STATES OF AMERICA
5   4   3   2

LIBRARY OF CONGRESS CATALOGING IN PUBLICATION DATA

Boulding, Maria.
    Gateway to hope.

    1. Failure (Christian theology)   2. Consolation.
I. Title.
BT730.5.B68   1987   248.4   87-4339
ISBN 0-932506-53-4

Contents

1

Only One Chance?

Alastair spent part of World War Two in the navy, a week of it in an open boat on the Atlantic, and the rest in a camp for prisoners of war in Germany. His return to a weary, drab, postwar Britain was something of an anticlimax, and he felt unable to settle back into an office routine. He dreamed of a more creative way of life in which he could make beautiful things. He was clever with his hands, and since childhood had been haunted by the beauty of shape and colour. He knew he had a flair for pottery, and against all economic common sense he decided to set up a craftsman's workshop. It was risky, but he was enthusiastic and hardworking, and he believed it could succeed. A few friends joined him, and with them he established a community where people could live a life of balanced wholeness in a Christian way, close to the earth and in a non-violent relationship to created things. They cared for one another and for those who came. Slowly the pottery began to thrive, and they had to build an extension.

Alastair poured his energy and love into the enterprise. He invested in it all the money he could lay hands on, all his time, his intelligence and his personal gifts. He worked and worked, giving the best years of his life to making it succeed, and it did. The work diversified, but the same integrity was found in every kind of product: the craftsmen gave to cups and plates, jugs and bowls, and the ordinary things people need for everyday life as much care as they gave to their more specialized items. Everything was done well, and so the artefacts of the place were beautiful. Some people caught a glimpse of uncreated Beauty through the beauty of these things fashioned with such honesty and love. There were hard times and disappointments, but the place survived because the founder was giving it his own life. As the years went by he became more and more identified with it. His dream came true, and it gave glory to God.

After many years a suspicion which had crossed Alastair's mind from time to time came to settle. The work was not going to survive him. He had thought of it as something which would live on after his death, as his contribution to the future. Most people leave children to carry on their name, but this craft-community was his brainchild, the repository of all his hopes. Now he was confronted with the truth he could no longer ignore, that among his colleagues there was no one who would be able to carry on the work once he was too old to continue. Perhaps he had built the thing too rigidly, so that it had been unable to adapt as they went along and was an anachronism already, although his personal prestige had masked the fact; perhaps economic or social conditions had changed so much that the need was no longer there to be met; perhaps it was simply that there was no one gifted and interested enough to be his heir apparent. Whatever the precise reason, he realized that the enterprise into which he had poured his life was going to die, and this not merely after his own death, as though others were going to dismantle it the day after his funeral, but even while he was still in full possession of his faculties but no longer of the strength and drive to make it work.

At first he could hardly bear to face the truth. He was tempted to deny the signs of the times, and to insist on shoring up the establishment at all costs. He could almost convince himself that he did not mind for his own sake but was concerned only for others: the work was valuable, and continuity must be kept. But he was too honest to keep up this pretence for long. In great pain he admitted to himself and others that the pottery would have to be phased out, and the community with it. He accepted its failure and allowed it to die. For himself too it was like a little death, in which he could see no meaning. Those who knew him well, however, recognized the last flowering of his courage and truthfulness, and saw in his own face the beauty he had sought to create.

If you have ever been sickened by the crumbling of some enterprise into which you had put all your best effort and the love of your heart, you are caught up into the fellowship of Christ's death and resurrection, whether or not you thought of your experience in that way. God has dealt with our failure by himself becoming a failure in Jesus Christ and so healing it from the inside. That is why we can meet him in our failure; it is a sure place for finding him, since he has claimed it. So central is failure to the Easter mystery that a person who had never grappled with it could scarcely claim to be Christ's friend and follower. It is the purpose of this book to explore the meaning of our failure in the light of his cross and resurrection.

Life in the Western world today tends to be success-oriented; from childhood we are exposed to influences which raise our expectations of ourselves or project on to us the expectations of others. In itself this is good, for when expectations grow from truth they can be very creative. If we had no expectations, and no one else expected any good of us either, we would sag and stagnate. Either we would never grow, or we would collapse under the struggles of life. Expectations can stretch us, challenging us to grow and to change, to try and to leap. When someone has enough faith in you to see your potential even when you are for the present defeated; when someone believes the best of you even though you are providing no evidence for it; when someone by persistently believing in you makes you believe in yourself, that person's expectations are highly creative. Moreover, the friend who knows you like that knows you at your most real, for the best is the truest in the end; our hearts are obstinately convinced of it.

The expectations which influence our lives are not always rooted in the truth, however. The energy and ingenuity of advertisers are directed to arousing a great many unreal expectations in the potential consumer. Some of us were puzzled in early youth by a certain dissimilarity between pictures on seed packets and what came up in our gardens. Many a young wife has been overwhelmed by a sense of failure when she compares the object she has taken out of the oven with the picture in the cookery book. The advertising industry continues to promise us a better standard of living, comfort, beauty, a cure, social success, more money, or the secret of staying young. When not fulfilled, these unreal expectations generate discontent, and make it more difficult for us to appreciate the real beauty and goodness in our lives.

This illusion can spread to more serious matters than a do-it-yourself kit or an infallible cure for the common cold. The cliché of the cinema is an image of romantic love which can arouse unreal expectations in young people, making them unable to appreciate a less than perfectly romantic partner and sending them into marriage looking for the wrong things. It can deceive them into falling in love with love, rather than with a real human being, and so trap them in a self-centred experience which has little to do with the self-giving of real love. Parents often have high expectations of their children, but if these are not the right expectations the children can feel that they are not appreciated or understood. They are made to feel that they have failed, when in truth it is only a set of unreal expectations that has prepared disappointment for the parents.

God knows us at our truest and therefore at our best. His expectations of us are creative in the proper sense. God loves us into growth and greatness; he gives us room to be ourselves, and appreciates us for what we are and what we can be. Our highest dreams of our own happiness and greatness are paltry things in comparison with what God plans for us. Ambition goes wrong when we fail to take his whole plan into our reckoning, or seek our glory apart from him; but we need the ambition which is grounded in truth. We need hope.

Hope is the dynamism of human beings, because we can dream dreams and see visions, and we know we are meant for a destiny not found as yet. Hope is the stretching of our will towards it, but hope includes an element of danger. We could fail, we could lose. If we were immunized against the risk of failure there would, literally, be no hope for us.

In the delicate, light control of a bird in flight, in the poise of a ballet dancer, in the fine sensitivity of a violinist, in the grace of an Olympic athlete – in all these and a thousand other brilliant skills there is a hair's breadth between glorious success and crashing failure. The very danger is part of the thrill. Half the failures in life arise from pulling in one's horse while he is leaping. No great actor is "safe"; each performance is a new risk, a new life, a new glory. It is unique, a new creation, and therefore it could fail. Balance is so delicate, so risky, so creative. In a nuance of the voice, or the choice of a word, or a movement of the hand, people express love, compassion, understanding, empathy; but they walk a tightrope between sentimentality and aloofness. It is good to risk, to try; and those who try sometimes fail.

Learning to deal with failure is part of life, a necessary part for those who aspire to be human. This is already obvious in everyday experience, before we attempt to plumb the depths of meaning that failure can disclose in our life with God. If you are learning to speak a new language you must sooner or later open your mouth and risk making a fool of yourself. It may be that gales of laughter will greet your remarks, but the hearers, when they recover, may point out your mistakes and you will have learned something. The same is true of a person learning to skate, or a young child learning to walk. They often fall, but if they did not they would never learn. Some failures act as a challenge, stimulating a person's aggressive instincts. We want to pick ourselves up again, fight back, try harder, direct our effort a little differently, and win next time.

This is especially the case in competitive situations, and it can be very healthy. Competitiveness in sport is the main challenge which calls out the best in us: skill, courage, endurance, generosity and a sense of fair play. In commerce and industry competitive prices and competitive standards provide the stimulus for growth and effort. Competitiveness can therefore be a good servant, but it is a bad master. When competitive instincts flourish in an appropriate context where people have a sane self-esteem and know that they are valuable and accepted, all is well; but in any group of people who share life together – whether a family or a religious community or a team of workers – community life suffers when people imagine that they have to succeed in order to justify their existence and make themselves acceptable. The constant need to go one better can be destructive of loving relationships in situations where truthful self-acceptance is more appropriate. If we cannot endure failing and being weak, and being seen to fail and to be weak, we are not yet in a position to love and be loved. The fear of failure and the illusion that we have to succeed in order to earn love can be a lifelong tyranny.

Sometimes it is possible to see in retrospect that a failure which grieved you at the time was a necessary stage on the way to something else. You fixed your hopes and ambitions on some career, some attainment, perhaps some relationship. Your efforts failed, and you were forced to look for something else: another job, a different career, another person to marry after the first engagement had broken down. If the first door had not shut against you, you would not have looked for a second; you would not have found your real destiny and your now much greater happiness.

Moreover, the very effort you put into seeking what you thought you wanted has stretched you and enlarged your capacity. The journey was already an experience, even if you never arrived at the goal you envisaged. Indeed, you may stumble upon a greater one. The seafaring explorers of the late fifteenth century sailed west looking for Cathay, India and the East. They failed – but they found the New World.

Positive reaction to failure may often be a process rather than an instantaneous response. At first the experience is so crushing that there seems to be nothing left at all, except sheer disappointment. There can be healing and recovery, but they take time. They may be furthered by a bath, a square meal, a good night's sleep or a talk with a friend.[1] Then you begin to pick up the pieces. The fruit of failure may be simply the discovery that we can fail, and survive; life is not finished because my cherished project has collapsed. The same discovery can be made when we are let down by other people or things: medical treatment fails to relieve your back pain, but in time you discover that you can live with it.

The fruits of failure need not be confined to one's own life. Most of us have known the extraordinary comfort of being understood in our weakness and failure by a compassionate friend, and it is usually from failing that the friend has learned compassion. Experience of failure can also make a person a good teacher, one who is sympathetic with the difficulties of learners.

All these examples are drawn from particular experiences which affect only part of our lives. There are larger "failures" affecting the whole person from which we suffer acutely, but which we recognize later as significant for our growth. What was experienced as a breakdown at the time may prove to have been a breakthrough. Creative disintegration is real, though not usually pleasant for its subject, as any butterfly emerging from its chrysalis might testify. So might many a human being who has come through psychological breakdown to a new wholeness.

Some experiences which feel like failures are nothing more than a discovery of one's own limitations. Many people, especially young people, dream unrealistically about what they are going to be or achieve. This may work for a time, because you can bridge the gap between dream and actuality by telling yourself that you have not yet had time to arrive; you have not yet had the lucky break or met the right people; or you need more practice. But one day the truth must be faced: "I am never going to achieve it, because it is not in me. I am not that sort of person. That is not my gift." This discovery is a moment of truth, and it is important to us as human beings and as followers of Christ that we accept the truth, however bitter. Truth is a freedom offered to us, a new freedom from illusion, a new freedom for a greater vision and a better dream. A door that God has shut (perhaps simply by making me the sort of person I am) means only a dead end closed off. I am invited to accept my limitations and allow God to work his dream for my life within them. We must see visions and dream dreams, but let them be the real ones, the dreams of true glory for which we were made.

So far we have thought about real failures which in the long run can be recognized as productive, and unreal failures which are only an exposure of our limitations. Over both we can be glad. This, however, is no more than a clearing of the ground before we tackle the real problems, for there are large areas of failure experienced in our own lives or recognized in the lives of others for which no such comforting explanation is available. Crushing, bitter, apparently meaningless failure darkens the lives of millions of people, and no simplistic solution will do. Before proceeding let us look at the picture.

People fail in their careers for a variety of reasons: they may be unable to adjust to galloping technology, or overtaken by the effects of economic recession, or considered "too old at forty". They are declared redundant – one of the cruellest phrases our society has minted. Behind these failed careers loom the misery and frustration of the long-term unemployed. For the hopeless poor of the world, the millions whose lives grind through unending want, failure is something different again, for they have never tasted the sweetness of any success at all.

Our educational and academic system too is a ladder of success, and many young people fall off it; they "can't measure up". Despite all the efforts made to broaden educational facilities and recognize the value of different gifts, some young people still feel they have failed. Yet perhaps this bites less deeply than a sense of failure where life's deepest relationships are concerned. Marital failure is not made lighter by its mounting frequency. Statistics are cold, but the reality behind them is a great number of wounded people who feel that they have more or less failed, or that someone has failed them, or both. Even in those marriages which remain stable there can be secret disillusionment, a failure to grow more deeply into the relationship after the first few years, a dull plodding on without growth in love. People trapped in this situation can feel themselves to be failures when they touch the edge of someone else's marriage, one in which husband and wife have never stopped growing over the years, and have grown together.

A poignant sense of failure can overcome a woman who suffers a miscarriage: she has not succeeded in cherishing the weak and vulnerable life entrusted to her. Similar feelings are suffered by both parents when they lose a young child; but the agonies of parental "failure" are not confined to families where the children die. Teenagers go wrong, young lives run into disaster, a seemingly unbridgeable gulf opens between the generations, and parents ask themselves, "Where did we fail?"

Or it may be social: the anguish of shyness, the inability to make friends, or habitual loneliness. Or the failure may be psychological: the feeling that "I can't cope" afflicts many normal people at some stage in their lives, but can be an abiding cause of suffering for those who are sick. Another cruel phrase used today designates some as "inadequate persons", but there is no one who does not at some time feel inadequate. The competitiveness of our culture generates feelings of inadequacy not only in the obvious senses already mentioned, but also in people who succeed in the rat race but fail as human beings. A man may make a great success of his business, but fail to maintain communication with his children.

From the moment we are born we begin to die, as a philosopher has said. If a favoured few insulate themselves, or are insulated by circumstances, against most of the common occasions of failure, they will probably have to face, sooner or later, the failure of strength and faculties that comes with ageing. Our ordinary language betrays it: "He's beginning to fail now." Everyone's organism will fail in the end, and so for all of us there is the prospect of ultimate failure: death.

Human experience of failure is so manifold that this list could be indefinitely prolonged, but enough has been said to suggest how prevalent are the kinds of failure which act not as a stimulus or challenge, but only as a bitter, crushing disappointment. A light goes out. The person does not get up and fight back, but is simply paralysed and apathetic. All the questions begin "Why . . .?" Self-esteem is lowered when we fail to correspond to the expectations of others, or our own, and people identify themselves accordingly: "I'm a failure; I'm no good at all." They can come to believe this, and then they suffer from loss of direction and meaning in their lives, and a feeling that everything is pointless.

This death of the spirit may be a process rather than the reaction of a moment. In the big commitments of life, whether a job or a marriage or a ministry, we give ourselves to a years-long project and obviously do not expect success all the time. There are ups and downs; but there is probably an over-all, half-conscious assessment of the project; we know whether, by and large, it is succeeding. If a deep security is there, as for instance in a stable marriage, the bad times can be weathered; but if an underlying conviction is growing in you that the thing is a failure, there is likely to be a last straw sooner or later, a failure which seems ultimate and irreparable because the cumulative experience is concentrated into this one moment.

Then, perhaps, you are in danger of sharing the widespread delusion that each of us has only one chance. Only one chance – and if you have wasted it, there is nothing more to be said.

*

We fail because we are weak, wounded, confused and inconsistent. We each have particular built-in weaknesses, flaws that seem to be part of the very stuff of our characters. We fail to do and we fail to be. We fail in the good we try to do, and we fail to love. At the deepest level of our life is sin: we fail God. This failure at the heart of our life with God is too big a subject for an introductory chapter and must be considered later, but for the moment two things can be said. The first is that here, here above all, is the place of failure where the God of our failures finds us with his grace. The second is that prayer is a relationship with him in which failure is tasted very bitterly, suffered with love, and allowed to become the place of resurrection. Prayer is an experience of failure at the heart of things, and here the mystery of Christ is operative in us, because Jesus himself is history's greatest failure.

From end to end the Bible tells the story of God's mercy in our need, his gifts in our emptiness, his power finding its scope to save where we are weak and helpless. At its centre stands the cross of Christ, in whom God became weak with us. Out of the failure and defeat of the crucified Jesus God snatched the victory of his love for us; or, more accurately, in the heart of that defeat the victory of love lay hidden, the victory that reveals itself in Christ risen and glorified. We listen to the story, and all the time we know another story, the story of our own inglorious lives, with their moments of joy and their dark failures. One story makes sense of the other; they are reciprocally illuminating. Yet to put it that way is not enough, for the truth is more wonderful. In some way the two stories are the same story. Your life is the latest chapter of the salvation history to which you listen in the Scriptures, its authentic prolongation, its necessary fulfilment. Christ fails in you and you fail in him; love conquers in you as it conquered in him, the love that is stronger than death.

This is the Good News. I fail now; not I, but Christ fails in me. Our gifts and our destitution, our strength and our weakness, our success and our failure, are taken up into Christ's holy living and sacrificial dying. He fully experienced them, and made of them an offering to God. They become part of the new risen life he lives and shares with us, the life which one day will transfigure our whole failing world. His resurrection is a process, a continuous transforming work in which all who belong to him have their necessary part to play by allowing the transformation to happen in themselves.

God's economy of cross and resurrection is sketched

already in the Old Testament. The next two chapters consider in this light first the successes and then the failures of some of his friends.

2

God's Friends Sometimes Succeed

The LORD sets no store by the strength of a horse
and takes no pleasure in a runner's legs;
his pleasure is in those who fear him,
who wait for his true love.

Psalm 147:10–11, NEB

In spite of this psalmist's reservations, the Old Testament was convinced that God could take delight in a runner's legs, as indeed in everything else he had created, for "behold, it was very good". The strong and the brave and the fleet of foot could wait for his true love as well as the weak and failing. Fear of the Lord was still possible amid success, and the Wisdom literature, especially the Book of Proverbs, provided abundant advice on how to combine them.

Ancient folklore, proverbs of the people, worldly wisdom and shrewd psychology are blended in Proverbs. The sages address young men particularly, giving useful hints on how to get on in life and avoid the pitfalls. Israelite wisdom is far removed from the speculative search of the Greeks. It is concerned with the practical affairs of life, but obedience to God's commandments is the indispensable foundation for handling one's affairs. Success is seen as his blessing. The typical young man who has been formed in this school is disciplined, intelligent, affable and pleasant in manner, prudent in his choice of friends, chary of loose-living women, just, capable and hardworking. He is a well brought up young man, whose manners and talents commend him in any company, and he believes in God.[1]

This could have remained an abstract ideal, but for the inclusion in Genesis of what may be fairly called a novel. Its hero is Joseph, whose adventures occupy chapters 37 to 50 of Genesis, and although the story is set far back in the patriarchal period (perhaps in about the eighteenth century BC), its psychological vividness derives from the Israelite wisdom which flourished under the monarchy, some eight or nine centuries later. Joseph is the kind of young man a sage would have liked to turn out, and although he has some bad experiences he passes through his suffering and humiliation to a successful career which saves many lives. The story unfolds very naturally, without the obvious divine interventions which characterized the lives of Abraham, Isaac and Jacob; but the whole human drama with its quota of weakness, folly and sin is guided by God and forms part of his providential plan for the Hebrew people.

The hero is not without his faults, and this makes him credible. Joseph is seventeen when we meet him, attractive, good-looking and a little spoilt, the youngest of a row of brothers and a trifle smug. He has grandiose dreams, and talks about them tactlessly:

> "Behold, we were binding sheaves in the field, and lo, my sheaf arose and stood upright; and behold, your sheaves gathered round it, and bowed down to my sheaf." His brothers said to him, "Are you indeed to reign over us? Or are you indeed to have dominion over us?" So they hated him yet more for his dreams and for his words.
>
> Genesis 37:7–8

There follows a similar dream about the sun and moon and eleven stars bowing to Joseph, which he recounts with the same lack of sensitivity, and their jealous hatred mounts to such a point that when he chances to fall into their hands far from home they attempt to murder him.

Joseph is pulled out alive from what should have been a deathtrap and soon finds himself a slave in Egypt. But "the LORD was with Joseph, and he became a successful man" (Genesis 39:2). He is the kind of person who falls on his feet and quickly makes himself indispensable, and his master entrusts him with extensive responsibility. His refusal of the adulterous advances of his master's wife lands him in further trouble, however, for her hatred secures his imprisonment. Joseph now seems to be at rock bottom: a foreigner with no rights, imprisoned on a false charge, apparently without trial or hope of redress. Yet again the narrator tells us that "the LORD was with Joseph and showed him steadfast love, and gave him favour in the sight of the keeper of the prison" (Genesis 39:21). Once more he becomes a trusted official, though still a prisoner.

His God-given skill in interpreting dreams eventually brings him out of gaol to a high place at court, and his sagacity in providing in advance for the years of famine saves Egypt from disaster. Joseph is now a top executive with everything at his command. He has conducted himself so wisely that he is rich, respected and very powerful. God has blessed him in every way. The only piece of unfinished business is reconciliation with his family, and when the misfortunes of famine at home bring them to seek food in Egypt, their unrecognized younger brother plays a curious cat-and-mouse game apparently designed to test them and remind them of their guilt. At the high pitch of dramatic tension there is recognition and repentance on the brothers' part; they are reconciled with Joseph and he points the moral:

> Do not be distressed, or angry with yourselves, because you sold me here; for God sent me before you to preserve life . . . to preserve for you a remnant on earth, and to keep alive for you many survivors. So it was not you who sent me here, but God . . . You meant evil against me, but God meant it for good, to bring it about that many people should be kept alive.
>
> Genesis 45:5,7–8; 50:20

It seems as though the whole affair was set up by God to ensure the survival of a clan which he will later build into his people, and to establish them in Egypt, whence he will powerfully rescue them a few centuries later. Yet even the hero, Joseph, brought trouble on himself by his youthful indiscretion; and his brothers, who were later regarded as the ancestors of the chosen people, made their sole contribution to this part of the story of salvation by murderous intentions and lying. God has used even human malice, given Joseph success against all the odds, and worked all things together for their good. God's will is done and his loving plans are furthered by the servants he calls, but with some admixture of human frailties and failures.

The chosen people spent the next few centuries in Egypt. Their faith probably became diluted during this time, and their memory of the patriarchs dim. In the first chapter of Exodus the atmosphere of familiarity with God seems to have been lost. Israel is to be called out of this situation of "sin" into a radically new situation of knowing God, but Egypt does not let them go without a struggle. Battle is joined between the desert-God of the Hebrews and the magicians of Egypt, behind whom stand the not-gods. The Nile is turned to blood; frogs swarm over Egypt; gnats hum; clouds of flies thicken; cattle die; people break out in boils; hail destroys crops and locusts the foliage; darkness enshrouds the Egyptians. The contest against Pharaoh's stubbornness is fought out until the tenth round. Then comes the climax:

Moses called all the elders of Israel, and said to them, "Select lambs for yourselves according to your families, and kill the passover lamb. Take a bunch of hyssop and dip it in the blood which is in the basin, and touch the lintel and the two doorposts with the blood . . .; and none of you shall go out of the door of his house until the morning. For the LORD will pass through to slay the Egyptians; and when he sees the blood on the lintel and on the two doorposts, the LORD will pass over the door, and will not allow the destroyer to enter your houses to slay you . . ." At midnight the LORD smote all the first-born in the land of Egypt . . . And Pharaoh rose up in the night, he, and all his servants, and all the Egyptians; and there was a great cry in Egypt, for there was not a house where one was not dead. And he summoned Moses and Aaron by night, and said, "Rise up, go forth from among my people, both you and the people of Israel; and go, serve the LORD, as you have said. Take your flocks and your herds . . . and be gone."

Exodus 12:21–23, 29–32

So they went, out into the dark and the desert, following God. Hasty arousal and hurrying off in the night to an unknown future have been the experience of thousands or even millions of people in modern times, when a knock comes on the door at midnight and someone is hustled off into a waiting car, and disappears. It has been for people in many parts of the world an experience of terror, but for the Israelites it was a high, heroic moment. Young children were probably sleepy and fretful, older ones shivering and excited. That spring night stamped the memory of God's people long ago, the night when they set off on a dark journey whose end they could not see. Indeed, we have not reached the end yet.

So crucial was this memory that under God's inspiration they enshrined it in an annual ritual, celebrating the night of their escape, the night when they began their long journey with God. We can hardly discern the historical kernel in stories which have become stylized after centuries of liturgical use, but one thing is clear: God's mighty act saved his people when they were helpless. He led them out from slavery, he led them through the sea and he took them to himself.

The desert journey lasted a symbolic forty years; perhaps this means "a generation". One of the odd things about it is that the distance to be covered was not very great, as the angel flies. The Israelites seem to have been wandering about fairly close to the promised land for a long time before they entered it, as we too are living our day-to-day lives and travelling towards our eternal home for so many years, when all the time it is so close to us that we can touch it if we will. Nevertheless they needed those forty years to get there; the

journey itself was vital because they could not live in the land
of promise without knowing the God who promised and gave
it.

During that long journey they did come to know him, the
Lord of the wilderness. They knew his care and tenderness
as he carried them and fed them with manna, and they knew
his holiness and his demand for their undivided fidelity.
Having brought Israel into a desert retreat where, because
ordinary comforts and securities were absent, he could
educate and provide for them, the Lord bound them to
himself in the unprecedented intimacy of a covenant:

> You have seen what I did to the Egyptians, and how I bore
> you on eagles' wings and brought you to myself. Now
> therefore, if you will obey my voice and keep my covenant,
> you shall be my own possession among all peoples . . . and
> you shall be to me a kingdom of priests and a holy nation.
>
> Exodus 19:4–6

Under the protection of his presence a remnant of them
survived the desert wandering and eventually took
possession of the promised land amid prodigies which
recalled those of the exodus a generation earlier. These are
God's mighty exploits; not a word of his promises had failed.
This was one side of the desert experience, the story of God's
success.

Entwined with it is a remarkably honest story of
remembered failures on the part of Israel. There must have
been high moments, times when they knew the power of God
carrying them; but there were certainly times when they lost
faith and were very much afraid. The cry, "Why did you
bring us out of Egypt to die in this wilderness?" begins to
make itself heard even before the crossing of the sea, and
runs like a refrain through the desert traditions. They fail
repeatedly to trust Yahweh, the Lord of the wilderness.
They grumble and rebel. They want to go back to Egypt,
even if it does mean slavery. They cease to want the land God
promises. Some of them disobey his orders about the manna;

some are seduced by idols. Almost on the threshold of the promised land they believe it impossible to conquer, and a fresh rebellion breaks out.

It was a strange honeymoon with God, but an essential and formative experience. Still ignorant of its destiny, Israel plumbed the depth of weakness, sin and failure, and in the process learned a little more about its God. This is why the desert experience never faded from Israel's memory. The desert had been the place of exposure to God, the place where in their failure his grace had triumphed.

One man bore the heavy human burden of responsibility for the whole enterprise, and its success was made possible by his faith. Moses had never aspired to be a leader or considered himself apt for the task; he had consented solely because God's will had been unmistakably clear. By the skin of their teeth the disorderly group of slaves had escaped from their masters, but in the desert Moses knew that the whole adventure often quivered on the brink of failure, and when the people grumbled he felt like a mother carrying a fractious child. He complained to the Lord:

> I am not able to carry this nation by myself alone; the weight is too much for me. If this is how you want to deal with me, I would rather you killed me!
>
> Numbers 11:14–15, JB

He was sometimes almost at breaking point, and his trust in God probably failed at times, but in weakness and dread he kept the people together, somehow. In the end he did not enter the land for which he had longed, the land which had been the focus of the Lord's promise and the people's hope, the land in which he, almost alone, had believed when they repeatedly lost faith. He died within sight of it, leaving the completion of the work to others, a humble servant who had felt himself weak with the weak, but had given the people inspired leadership throughout the most crucial adventure of their history. Against all the odds, it had succeeded. Through him, the Lord's will prospered.

One of the most remarkable and best-loved parts of the Old Testament is the story of a man who was an amazing success in all his undertakings, but whose life was marred by a failure of love. David was the darling of Israel and the darling of God. He was not born to power or ready-made success; when Samuel came looking for the one destined to be the Lord's Anointed, Jesse did not at first even bring David forward with his other seven sons, having apparently never thought of this youngest one as a potential leader. David was a boy "of fresh complexion, with fine eyes and pleasant bearing" (1 Samuel 16:12, JB); these are slender assets, but he was also courageous and resourceful, and he knew and loved the Lord.

Legends cluster round his youth. He was David the Giant-Killer; he was the loyal friend of Jonathan; his bravery and skill in battle caused the people to sing as the army returned, "Saul has killed his thousands, and David his tens of thousands." His successes aroused Saul's jealousy, and after several narrow escapes from the murderous assaults of the increasingly neurotic king he was forced to flee. David seemed to have lost all that his courage and the blessing of the Lord had brought him, but during his time as a fugitive he endeared himself to his followers while maintaining his reverence for the king's sacred office. He would not seize the kingship, but when Saul was played out it fell to him by the manifest will of the Lord.

As king, David went from strength to strength. He was not only a warrior but also a man of political sagacity. He built up a ring of vassal states round Israel, united the divided tribes within his people, captured the strategic city of Jerusalem and made it at once a political and a religious capital, won fame as a poet and musician, married various wives and begot children. Everything was his. He was brave, and generous to his enemies. In his relationship with the Lord he was trusting and trusted. Every story about David reveals him as spontaneous, robust and fully human. He was a man who lived and loved.

At the height of his success David conceived the idea of

building a house for the Lord who had blessed him so richly. It seemed a good idea and was approved at first by the prophet Nathan, his adviser, but the Lord had other plans, and his word came to David through Nathan next day:

> Would you build me a house to dwell in? . . . I have been with you wherever you went, and have cut off all your enemies from before you; and I will make for you a great name . . . I will raise up your offspring after you, who shall come forth from your body, and I will establish his kingdom. He shall build a house for my name, and I will establish the throne of his kingdom for ever. I will be his father, and he shall be my son.
>
> 2 Samuel 7:5, 9, 12–14

David's project has to die; he is not to achieve his ambition of building a house for the Lord. But the Lord has something much greater in store; he will himself build for David a "house" in the sense of an abiding dynasty, in which the ancient hopes of Israel will come to be focused. The perspectives are open towards a fulfilment of this promise in one of David's line who will be God's Son in a more than adoptive sense.

This is the greatest of all the blessings God has showered upon David, and the king's humble prayer is a fine example of the gratitude of a successful man who has remained open to the Giver of all he enjoys:

> Who am I, O Lord GOD, and what is my house, that thou hast brought me thus far? And yet this was a small thing in thy eyes, O Lord GOD; thou hast spoken also of thy servant's house for a great while to come! . . . And what more can David say to thee? Because of thy promise, and according to thy own heart, thou hast wrought all this greatness . . . Therefore thou art great, O LORD God; for there is none like thee.
>
> 2 Samuel 7:18–22

From this height David fell by sin. The account in 2 Samuel 11 and the following chapters is of great interest, both because of the honesty with which the episode of adultery and murder in the life of Israel's ideal monarch was remembered, and because of the deep sense of sin which it reveals. David had been trusted by God with every kind of favour and success. He had risen to the height of his powers because God had consistently blessed him, and he had lived in God's close friendship. Now he failed, but not in an enterprise. He failed a Person. He had loved, and now he betrayed the one he loved.

Nathan may have been taking a risk when he confronted David with the wrong he had done, for the king's attempted cover-up might have extended to inconvenient prophets too. He went about it very skilfully, putting before David a story which took the king off his guard and forced him to see the ugly reality of his own conduct. Nathan said to David:

> "There were two men in a certain city, the one rich and the other poor. The rich man had very many flocks and herds; but the poor man had nothing but one little ewe lamb, which he had bought. And he brought it up, and it grew up with him and with his children; it used to eat of his morsel, and drink from his cup, and lie in his bosom, and it was like a daughter to him. Now there came a traveller to the rich man, and he was unwilling to take one of his own flock or herd to prepare for the wayfarer who had come to him, but he took the poor man's lamb, and prepared it for the man who had come to him." Then David's anger was greatly kindled against the man; and he said to Nathan, "As the LORD lives, the man who has done this deserves to die . . ." Nathan said to David, "You are the man."
>
> 2 Samuel 12:1–5, 7

A powerful novel or play can do the same for any of us; the story can carry us away and show us the truth about ourselves. We know the inside story of our own lives, but we can grow insensitive or refuse to face the reality of it; or perhaps we are simply too weary and preoccupied to see it. Another story is laid alongside our own, and the effect is overwhelming. Each story illuminates the other. These tactics were remarkably effective with David, who was a man of too much insight and honesty to dissemble any longer. In his repentance he was not concerned for his public image, or even for the objective norm of morality by which he had failed to measure his actions. He went straight to the heart of the matter: "I have sinned against the LORD." I have failed in the fullest sense, failed a person, failed the LORD.

David is an extraordinary character, even in the paradoxical sense that he is extraordinarily typical. In his success as a king after God's own heart he was a vital part of the preparation for God's reign on earth; in his failure he typified human persons blessed and loved by God, capable of greatness but deeply wounded and calling for redemption. His sin was a turning point: he was forgiven, but disasters multiplied in his family. David accepted his misfortunes magnanimously, but the time of high success was over, and the near-contemporary sources on which this history is based recall his pathetic old age.

The Old Testament habitually has second thoughts, however, and many further thoughts on David. A eulogy which was delivered centuries later by Ben Sira (Sirach 47:2–11) has much to say about David's heroic exploits. His giant-killing and his ten thousands, his victories and the liturgical creativity credited to him are generously remembered, but only one brief line alludes to the darker side, and then simply to record forgiveness: "The Lord took away his sins." We might think this eulogy inflated, hyperbolic and biased. Perhaps it is, but God is biased in the way he looks at our lives. It is only we who brood over our sins. God does not brood over them; he dumps them at the bottom of the sea (cf. Micah 7:19). The only thing that we are ordered to commemorate under the new covenant is Christ's redemption.

When God absolves, it is not a mere amnesty or remission of punishment, but something absolute, as the word "absolve" implies, a total setting free. His forgiveness of our failures re-creates us in his love, so that we are as beautiful in his sight as his creative dream would have us. He sees only the lovely things in our lives; or perhaps it would be truer to say that he sees our sins and wounds and failures as lovely, because transfigured.

Success and failure came in different shapes to God's friends during the Old Testament period. In a time of widespread apostasy from the God of Israel, when the idolatrous cult of Baal flourished under the patronage of Queen Jezebel, Elijah arose as a lonely champion of the truth. His word was powerful. He induced a drought, worked miracles for sundry deserving cases, and successfully evaded royal search parties sent to deal with him. Then he flung down his challenge: singlehanded, in the power of his God, he would take on the four hundred prophets of Baal in a contest on Mount Carmel. Two bulls are to be slain, but not set alight. Each side shall pray, and let the best god win. The prophets of Baal pray, dance, mutilate and lash themselves into a frenzy, but nothing happens. Elijah taunts them, but their god does not reply. Now it is time for Elijah's innings, and he gives it maximum dramatic effect:

> He said, "Fill four jars with water, and pour it on the burnt offering, and on the wood." And he said, "Do it a second time"; and they did it a second time. And he said, "Do it a third time"; and they did it a third time. And the water ran round about the altar, and filled the trench also with water . . . And Elijah the prophet came near and said, "O LORD, God of Abraham, Isaac and Jacob, let it be known this day that thou art God in Israel, and that I am thy servant, and that I have done all these things at thy word. Answer me, O LORD, answer me, that this people may know that thou hast turned their hearts back."
>
> 1 Kings 18:33–37

He is setting it up in such a way as to make the miracle as difficult as possible, that God's power may be the more clearly seen. He is taking a fearful risk, for he will not simply look a fool if God does not vindicate him; he will probably be torn limb from limb by his exulting opponents. He knows that God will not let him down; he trusts him, and it is a spectacular success:

> The fire of the LORD fell, and consumed the burnt offering, and the wood, and the stones, and the dust, and licked up the water that was in the trench. And when all the people saw it, they fell on their faces; and they said, "The LORD, he is God; the LORD, he is God." And Elijah said to them, "Seize the prophets of Baal; let not one of them escape." And they seized them; and Elijah brought them down to the brook Kishon, and killed them there.
>
> 1 Kings 18:38–40

Elijah has had his big moment and won the tournament by the power of God, but it has drained him. He is a strong, zealous man, but even the strong have their times of weakness. He retires to the desert, partly to flee from the vengeance of Jezebel but mainly to renew his contact with the source of his people's faith in communion with the Lord who chose Israel and covenanted with them in the wilderness. There under a broom bush he suffers a nervous collapse: he feels a failure, notwithstanding his recent triumph: "LORD, I have had enough. Take my life; I am no better than my ancestors" (1 Kings 19:4, JB). God strengthens him with a gift of food, as he strengthened Israel with manna long ago, and Elijah walks for forty days in that strength, to the holy mountain of the covenant. There on the mountain, outside a cave, he comes to know God in a new way:

> The word of the LORD came to him, and he said to him . . . "Go forth, and stand upon the mount before the LORD." And behold, the LORD passed by, and a great

and strong wind rent the mountains, and broke in pieces the rocks before the LORD, but the LORD was not in the wind; and after the wind an earthquake; but the LORD was not in the earthquake; and after the earthquake a fire, but the LORD was not in the fire; and after the fire a still small voice. And when Elijah heard it, he wrapped his face in his mantle and went out and stood at the entrance to the cave.

1 Kings 19:9, 11–13

Wind, storm, earthquake and fire had been traditional accompaniments of God's self-manifestations, their power evoking his transcendence. Now he transcends the mighty signs themselves. Perhaps Elijah needed the experience of his own weakness to prepare him for this new revelation; it may be that he was more open to the mystery of God now than in the exhilaration of his victory on Carmel. Like Israel of old, he learned God anew in the desert.

Centuries after Elijah another man in the prophetic tradition presents the interplay of success and failure in a way which is at once delicately humorous and full of insight into the mercy of God. The story of Jonah is probably inspired fiction, a little gem of satire directed against the narrowness of post-exilic Judaism which, turned in on itself, needed to be reminded of God's universal saving love. The hero, if hero he can be called, is a Hebrew prophet, but throughout the beautifully constructed story he appears in an unfavourable light, whereas the various gentile characters behave with consistent decency. In Scene One Jonah is called by the Lord to preach in Nineveh, the capital of brutal, pagan Assyria, which to the Israelite mind was the epitome of gentile wickedness. Jonah refuses and heads as fast as possible in the opposite direction to escape the Lord. This plan is thwarted, because a storm at sea leads to Jonah's exposure as a fugitive from the Lord, and the pagan sailors, after praying to the Lord and with sincere regret, find themselves with no alternative but to drop Jonah overboard. The Lord, however, has abandoned neither Jonah nor his original intention, and he makes use of a co-operative whale to return Jonah to his point of departure. Now, half-way through the story, Jonah is back at square one, and the command is reiterated: "Go and preach in Nineveh."

In no very sweet temper Jonah complies, proclaiming the doom of the city: "In forty days' time Nineveh will be destroyed!" He derives some satisfaction from the prospect, and retires to a safe distance to watch. The Ninevites, however, have been touched by grace. They take the word of the Lord seriously and set themselves to penance, co-opting even the animals into the national effort of conversion and repentance. God also "repents" on seeing it, and lifts the sentence. Jonah, camping outside the city in discomfort from the heat and misery of his general situation, is disgusted at this turn of events: his preaching has been a success, and he wishes it had not. He grows angry with the Lord who has failed to vindicate his prophecy of doom, flinging back at him the beautiful, ancient words in which the Lord himself had disclosed his love to Moses: "This, O LORD, is what I feared when I was in my own country, and to forestall it I tried to escape to Tarshish; I knew that thou art 'a god gracious and compassionate, long-suffering and ever constant, and always willing to repent of the disaster'" (Jonah 4:2, NEB).

This is prayer indeed; the Hebrew tradition of prayer is nothing if not honest, and the ugliness of Jonah's malice and resentment pours out before the Lord, accusing his very love and mercy of disappointing Jonah's hopes of revenge. We almost expect a heavenly missile to flatten the near-blasphemous Jonah as, like Elijah, he moans that he has had enough. But no, God answers him with sweet reasonableness. God is laughing at Jonah, but how gently:

> "Are you so angry?" . . . "Yes," he answered, "mortally angry." The LORD said . . . "And should not I be sorry for the great city of Nineveh, with its hundred and twenty thousand who cannot tell their right hand from their left, and cattle without number?"
>
> Jonah 4:9–11, NEB

Jonah failed to obey the Lord in the first instance, and failed throughout the mission to understand him. In bitterness of spirit, with dispositions highly unsuitable to any emissary of the Lord, he preached with astounding, and unwelcome, success. The success was followed by a breakdown, in which the sin of his own heart was laid bare in an encounter with the Lord who revealed himself as tender, merciful and humorous. This was Jonah's moment of truth. The maturity of this piece of story-telling suggests much about the faith of obscure Israelites, and the insight it gave them into the heart of God.

The successes and failures of God's Old Testament friends so far considered have been those of men, since it was generally men who led the people, exercised royal power or served as prophets, though there were exceptional women like Deborah. There was one particular instance of failure which afflicted women; it is significant not only because of its plangent recurrence throughout the Old Testament, but also because it points towards the mystery of the New.

The ability to bear and rear many sons was the principal sign of God's blessing in the life of a woman, sterility her most bitter failure. We need not refer this preoccupation with fertility directly to the coming of the Messiah, for most of the time people were not thinking precisely of that. More prominent was the conviction that the primary way in which a man survived after death was by prolonging his life in his children and grandchildren; the blotting out of his name from Israel would be a tragedy. A barren wife meant the withholding of this blessing, and could even be the sign of a curse. The grief and humiliation of sterile women rise in heartbroken cries to the Lord of life; and time after time, where there is faith, obedience and openness to his promise, the childless bear children and mourning is turned to joy. The song attributed to Hannah articulates the thanksgiving of others:

My heart exults in the LORD;
my strength is exalted in the LORD.

My mouth derides my enemies,
because I rejoice in thy salvation . . .
The bows of the mighty are broken,
but the feeble gird on strength.
Those who were full have hired themselves out for bread,
but those who were hungry have ceased to hunger.
The barren has borne seven,
but she who has many children is forlorn.
The LORD kills and brings to life;
he brings down to Sheol and raises up.
The LORD makes poor and makes rich;
he brings low, he also exalts.

1 Samuel 2:1, 4–7

Behind Hannah stand Sarah, Rebekah, Rachel, the mother of Samson and many another woman who felt herself a failure. Their failure became the place of entry for the Lord, who overturns our scale of values and gives life out of death. As his word brings them fruitfulness their triumphant child-bearing unites them with the mystery of salvation; they sing with the victorious warriors and the vindicated poor.

Women of today who long for children are not the only people who can recognize themselves in these once-barren mothers. All of us, men and women, know the anguish of sterility at times. We may have to speak, counsel, guide or write, yet feel empty and devoid of all inspiration. Most of us know the feeling of complete helplessness when someone we love is hurt or bereaved or shattered by some disaster; we long to comfort but there seems to be nothing we can do or say. Anyone whose life and work mean continual giving is sharply aware of the times when we seem to have nothing in us to give, no life to share, nothing to communicate. In these experiences we can only open our barrenness to the Lord of life, and believe that we, like Hannah and many another, are caught up into a mystery of life given where there was only death. The spiritual heirs of these Old Testament heroines people Luke's infancy narrative, where Zechariah and Elizabeth look like Abraham and Sarah thinly disguised, and

Mary's *Magnificat* takes up Hannah's song in a still more joyful key. Mary was not sterile but virgin; her virginity was an emptiness, a poverty, a place of no life, but an availability to God. The weak things of this world he chooses, to shame the strong. It is a pattern that will recur in her Son.

*

The Old Testament provides a portrait gallery of God's friends, in whose lives success and failure are paired as necessarily as light with shadow. Some of them emerge from obscurity, like Joseph and David, and enjoy great success as a result of God's blessing on their hard work. They remain open to God in the midst of success, and play an essential role in his care for his people. In other lives there is an alternation between successful work and failure, and it may be in the latter that the strong come to know God more closely; this was possibly true of Elijah. For others again humiliation and the sense of personal failure were habitual. In the case of Moses the work of God went forward none the less.

Another kind of failure marks the lives of those who, bound in love to God, betray him. They fail the Lord, like Israel in the desert and David at the height of his prosperity; but the Lord does not fail them, and in their weakness they find grace and mercy. No single one of the great men and women of the Old Testament is flawless. They are a mixture of strength and weakness, as we all are. They all fail in some way, but through God's fidelity to them they live and love and make their souls. With many a setback, the work goes on.

3

Prophetic Failure

From most of the stories recalled in the preceding chapter we could simply conclude that while God's friends sometimes succeed and sometimes fail, all their experience can be used by God. They are caught up in his designs of love and entrusted with his gifts; they use their wisdom and strength in his service and they enjoy varying measures of success, remaining open to their empowering God. They all prove themselves inadequate at times, but God's work continues. Human failures, including culpable failures, are woven into the texture of his story and used for its furtherance in such a way that with benefit of hindsight we can see that more good came from human frailties than could have resulted from a smooth, unhindered fulfilment of the plan. God works all things together unto good for those whom he has called.

Even within the Old Testament, however, the mystery of failure is plumbed more deeply than this. The optimistic religious humanism of the Wisdom tradition, which found expression in the novel about Joseph, is by no means the last word. Other discoveries awaited God's friends, especially those within the prophetic tradition. The prophets suffered failure at its most bitter when they found themselves unable to speak to the heart of their people the word entrusted to them by the Lord, yet failure was often explicitly built into their mission. The powerful word of the Lord was given to them, and along with it the certainty that the people would not listen. Many a prophet was not merely a failure but a programmed failure. Only by failing could he do the Lord's work, yet his failure was no less painful for that.

This seems to have been the experience of Hosea, Isaiah

and Jeremiah, and in some sense that of the mysterious Servant of the Lord who appears in the later parts of the Book of Isaiah. The present chapter is concerned with it because it points directly to the mystery of Jesus Christ, the Servant who conquered through failure, whose love is victorious in our lives not simply in spite of our failures but through them.

Hosea's story is that of a failed marriage.[1] He is ordered by God to marry a woman who bears him three children, and to give these children symbolic names which suggest a crescendo of condemnation and anger. The woman is unfaithful and Hosea finds himself a cuckold, yet though discarded he still loves her. He brings her back and keeps her under close guard, depriving her of recourse to the lovers who seduced her and the amenities and riches they provided; she is to be his alone in a solitude which, though austere, will be the place where love is reborn. His stratagem of tenderness leads to a reconciliation, and their marriage is renewed through the power of his faithful, persevering love. He will provide her with all the blessings she sought elsewhere, and she will come at last to know him.

Hosea's marital suffering is a lived parable of the relationship between the Lord and his people Israel. At Sinai in the desert the marriage covenant had been sealed between them, but after Israel's entry into the promised land the temptations of the local gods proved too strong. Israel had come in from the wilderness and had to adjust to a settled, agricultural way of life, and the new way had to be learned amid a pagan Canaanite people for whom the cycle of the seasons and the fertility of field, flock and herd was bound up with the nature-gods, the "baalim". The prophets denounced Israelite recourse to the baalim as adultery: it was an infidelity to the Lord, Israel's Bridegroom, and the image was all the stronger in that Canaanite worship, being concerned also with human fertility, sometimes involved ritual prostitution. Hosea knew that love and wrath contended in God's heart, and envisaged a symbolic return to the wilderness as the only solution. Israel must be stripped

of all the gifts of the fertility-gods; she must journey back to
the place of first love, and learn to see the Lord as the author
of all her blessings. She must come to know him through the
creative, re-educative love he bears her:

> She says, "I will go after my lovers;
> they give me my food and drink,
> my wool and flax, my oil and my perfumes."
> Therefore I will block her road with thorn-bushes,
>   and obstruct her path with a wall,
> so that she can no longer follow her old ways.
> When she pursues her lovers she will not overtake them,
>   when she looks for them she will not find them;
>   then she will say,
> "I will go back to my husband again;
>   I was better off with him than I am now."
> For she does not know that it is I who gave her
>   corn, new wine, and oil,
>   I who lavished upon her silver and gold
>   which they spent on the Baal.
>   Therefore I will take back
> my corn at the harvest and my new wine at the vintage,
>   and I will take away the wool and the flax.
>
> Hosea 2:5–9, NEB

But this deprivation is not a mere punishment; it is a
summons to a place of unprecedented intimacy and new
hope. The desert will be empty only because the gods that
came between the Lord and his people will have disappeared,
for he will go into the wilderness with her, and his love will
be her whole life.

An ill-omened name appears in the prophecy, the Valley
of Achor, or of "Misfortune" or "Trouble"; it was a place
haunted by the memory of a sin committed at the time when
Joshua and the Israelites were conquering the land, and of
its fearful punishment (cf. Joshua 7:16–26). This too is to be
transformed into a place of opportunity and new life:

Behold, I will allure her,
　　and bring her into the wilderness,
　　and speak tenderly to her.
And there I will give her her vineyards,
　　and make the Valley of Achor a door of hope.
And there she shall answer as in the days of her
　　　　youth,
　　as at the time when she came out of the land of
　　　　Egypt . . .
And I will betroth you to me in righteousness and in
　　　　justice,
in steadfast love, and in mercy.
I will betroth you to me in faithfulness;
and you shall know the LORD.

Hosea 2:14–15, 19–20

The place of failure is to become a door of hope; the desert
where Israel sinned is to be the place for knowing God. Many
of us have some haunted place in our lives. It may be a
geographical place, or a situation, or a relationship, or a job.
Once, long ago, we failed there, and now we are afraid to go
back, afraid of the echoes that the place awakens for us. But
God may want to take us back there, to come with us into
the place of our bad memories so that he can heal them.
Hosea must have known better than we do what the desert
experience had been like for Israel: not much fidelity on their
side and a great deal of hunger, thirst, fear, rebellion,
weariness and failure. Yet he could assert that some re-
establishment of that bleak experience would be a chance for
coming closer to God. In the place of remembered failure
Israel would "know the LORD" in that deep, biblical sense
of "knowing" which evokes the love of man and wife in
tender, mutual possession.

Hosea had discovered the truth he was preaching in the
anguish and humiliation of his own failed marriage, even
though it seems that his story had a happy ending. God
makes himself known to us through the experiences of our
lives, and it is the greatness of Hosea that he had a heart

tender and ardent enough to serve as God's instrument in this vital stage of revelation. Evil is not to prevail in the end, because God's heart is greater than our failures. God casts himself in the role of the discarded lover, waiting and longing, and comes with us into our wilderness, to suffer through it with us and there make us understand his love.

When Isaiah is called to be a prophet it seems as though his mandate to speak the Lord's word is given simultaneously with a prediction of its failure. Isaiah is in the temple; his vision of God is one of the most solemn and numinous scenes of the Old Testament; there is an overwhelming sense of God's holiness; Isaiah responds with obedient faith; and yet the end is sombre:

> I heard the voice of the Lord saying:
> "Whom shall I send? Who will be our messenger?"
> I answered, "Here I am, send me." He said:
> "Go, and say to this people,
> 'Hear and hear again, but do not understand;
> see and see again, but do not perceive.'
> Make the heart of this people gross,
> its ears dull;
> shut its eyes,
> so that it will not see with its eyes,
> hear with its ears,
> understand with its heart,
> and be converted and healed."

Isaiah 6:8–10, JB

If this is to be taken as a simple, literal account of what happened, it means that Isaiah undertook his task of preaching for more than forty years knowing from the outset that it would fail. This seems so unlike God's way of dealing with human beings that perhaps we should understand it differently. The story of Isaiah's vocation may have been given its final form late in his life, and been coloured by the experience of his maturity.

As a young man he leapt eagerly to receive the Lord's command: "Here I am, send me." With a burning coal from the holy altar he was cleansed, with the fire of the very holiness of God. He set out with hope, enthusiasm and the ardent love he had caught from the Holy One of Israel. He laboured and preached throughout a long prophetic career, listening again and again to the word and trying to get Judah and Jerusalem to listen to it amid the vicissitudes of wars and political reshuffles in the eighth century BC. For the most part the people did not listen, because Isaiah's demand for unconditional trust and faith in the Lord was not generally thought to be politically realistic. Towards the end of his life Isaiah wrote as his personal testament:

> They are a rebellious people, lying sons,
> sons who will not hear the instruction of the LORD;
> who say to the seers, "See not";
>   and to the prophets, "Prophesy not to us what is right;
>   speak to us smooth things, prophesy illusions . . .
>   let us hear no more of the Holy One of Israel."
>
> Isaiah 30:9–11

This is the voice of bitter experience; Isaiah has tried and failed. Yet there are enough indications in his book of his own deep faith and trust in the Lord, whose quiet presence was like the waters of Shiloah that flowed in tranquillity, for us to guess that in old age he could look back on what seemed to be a career of failure, and know in the deep peace of his heart that the failure had been part of God's plan. God did not will the people's obduracy, but he had foreknown it and still loved them. In some way his plans would go forward, even if only a remnant were saved to form the stock of the new people and inherit the future.

Isaiah may never have understood more than this; he may have lived and died with the "Why?" question unanswered, content to leave it to God. We cannot fathom the mystery of God's love either, but we have the advantage of a longer perspective and can see something of why failure was not an accident but intrinsic to a prophet's calling.

Israel was the people of the word, the people created and formed by God to listen. His "word" to them was an experience of his mighty, saving deeds as well as his spoken message, and the two always interlocked. They knew the Lord as he led them, saved them, judged, punished, forgave and cherished them; and they knew him because his message was spoken by a series of prophets who stood close to him and listened, and interpreted for them the Lord's purposes. A prophet was therefore a man (or occasionally a woman) who both emerged from the people and was sent to speak to them. We commonly think of him as the one sent to Israel bearing the Lord's message, and so he was; but he also himself was Israel, the embodiment of his people, a listener amid a people who should have been listening, a man whose whole soul was claimed by God and nurtured by the traditions of God's people. The prophet addressed Israel, standing over against it; but he also had to experience in himself the reality of Israel, allowing himself to stand as a sign of what Israel truly was.

This could be fearfully demanding, because there were times when the people did not want to know the truth of things and hated the prophet who reminded them. A description of Judah devastated for its sins occurs early in Isaiah:

O sinful nation, people loaded with iniquity,
race of evildoers, wanton destructive children
    who have deserted the LORD,
    spurned the Holy One of Israel . . .
  Where can you still be struck
    if you will be disloyal still?
    Your head is covered with sores,
    your body diseased;
from head to foot there is not a sound spot in you –
nothing but bruises and weals and raw wounds
  which have not felt compress or bandage or soothing oil.
                  Isaiah 1:4–6, NEB

This poem may well have been composed in a time of material devastation, perhaps during the war of 735 BC, but the prophet saw through the external calamities of Judah to the inner rottenness they symbolized: "From head to foot there is not a sound spot in you." This, he maintained, was the truth about his people's condition, a truth forced upon them in time of national disaster but denied in days of prosperity when complacency reigned. Isaiah's personal suffering, his anguish and failure, were the counterpart of this national sickness; Judah would deny it and maintain that all was well, but the prophet lived with the truth and agonized over it. Because he was not merely sent to the people but identified with them, he could not stand aloof or confine himself to condemning their sin; he had to suffer it with them and in some degree take it upon himself.

Prophetic participation in the people's sick condition is no more than hinted in Isaiah's story, but for Jeremiah about a century later it was a central experience. Judah had in the meantime gone from bad to worse under corrupt kings, but along with inner decay went a yet more determined complacency. Nothing could go wrong, all was well, the survival of the nation and the present regime was guaranteed by the temple in Jerusalem, where the Lord dwelt. So ran the official doctrine, bolstered by court prophets, the yes-men employed to give religious sanction to the king's policies.

Jeremiah was young when the Lord's irruption into his life set him aside to be a true prophet, but he had been a marked man since before his birth:

> The word of the LORD came to me saying,
> "Before I formed you in the womb I knew you,
> and before you were born I consecrated you;
> I appointed you a prophet to the nations."
>
> Jeremiah 1:4–5

Jeremiah did not leap to the task as Isaiah had done; he was more like Moses, shrinking from a role for which he felt himself inadequate:

> I said, "Ah, Lord GOD! Behold, I do not know how to
> speak, for I am only a youth." But the LORD
> said to me,
> "Do not say, 'I am only a youth',
> for to all to whom I send you you shall go,
> and whatever I command you you shall speak.
> Be not afraid of them,
> for I am with you to deliver you."
>
> Jeremiah 1:6–8

He was reluctant from the first, and things did not grow easier with practice. In the Lord's name he was sent to disabuse a complacent people, to reveal that their confidence in the temple was self-delusion because their conduct made a mockery of their covenant with the Lord. The temple would not save them, for it would be swept away when God's wrath fell on them, as once long ago his shrine at Shiloh had been destroyed. Armies were coming from the north, and the people would be killed or deported.

Afraid, reluctant, habitually shrinking from his mission but constrained by the word he bore, Jeremiah exposed the rottenness of society. Judah was not merely sick now, as in Isaiah's day; it was past curing:

> The wound of the daughter of my people wounds me too,
> all looks dark to me, terror grips me.
> Is there not balm in Gilead any more?
> Is there no doctor there?
> Then why does it make no progress,
> this cure of the daughter of my people?
>
> Jeremiah 8:21–22, JB

Judah's case was hopeless, and Jeremiah's duty was to say so, to grieve and lament and mourn for a people dead and corrupt in its very heart, a people he loved. His was a ministry of grief, because Judah was dead:

> Summon the wailing women to come,
>   send for the women skilled in keening
> to come quickly and raise a lament for us,
>   that our eyes may run with tears
>   and our eyelids be wet with weeping . . .
> Death has climbed in through our windows,
>   it has entered our palaces,
> it sweeps off the children in the open air
>   and drives young men from the streets.
>
> Jeremiah 9:17–18, 21, NEB

It is too late for repentance, and in any case repentance is a moral impossibility:

> Can the Nubian change his skin,
>   or the leopard his spots?
> And you? Can you do good,
>   you who are schooled in evil?
>
> Jeremiah 13:23, NEB

It would take a miracle to change Judah's corrupt heart. But the greatness of Jeremiah is that amid the almost unrelieved gloom of his life and ministry he believed in such a miracle and foretold it. The most enduring part of his message is the promise that the old covenant, violated beyond repair from the side of the human partner, will be superseded by a new covenant in which God himself will be the author of his people's faithfulness by creating for man a new heart:

> Behold, the days are coming, says the LORD, when I will make a new covenant with the house of Israel and the house of Judah . . . I will put my law within them, and I will write it upon their hearts; and I will be their God, and they shall be my people. And no longer shall each man

teach his neighbour and each his brother, saying, "Know
the LORD", for they shall all know me, from the least of
them to the greatest . . . for I will forgive their iniquity,
and I will remember their sin no more.

Jeremiah 31:31, 33–34

There were flashes of this kind for Jeremiah, moments of
vision in which he saw beyond the present disasters to some
unprecedented act of God; but for the time being his daily,
terrible work was to proclaim that there was no future. Judah
was dead, and nothing whatever in the contemporary scene
offered any hope, any opening towards life or a future for the
established order. He saw the imminent Babylonian invasion
as a just punishment to which they must submit. Violently
he preached non-violence.

It was not enough merely to say all this; Jeremiah had to
be a living symbol of the truth he proclaimed. Sensitive and
tender-hearted, he must have longed for marriage and family
life, but he was commanded to remain celibate. Like any
Israelite he knew that marriage and child-rearing were God's
gift to humankind, but they were out of place in that context
of death. In normal circumstances it might be possible for an
Israelite to hope that by leaving children to carry on his name
he would prolong his life into the future. But now there was
no future, and so it was no time for marrying:

The word of the LORD came to me: "You shall not marry
a wife; you shall have neither son nor daughter in this place
. . . In your own days, in the sight of you all, and in this
very place, I will silence all sounds of joy and gladness, and
the voice of bridegroom and bride."

Jeremiah 16:1–2, 9, NEB

It is not surprising that the message which Jeremiah both
spoke and embodied in his own person was unacceptable.
The people did not want to know, and clashes with the court
prophets were inevitable. Jeremiah denounced them as lying

impostors who covered up the agonizing but entirely necessary truth of the nation's condition:

> From prophet to priest,
> everyone deals falsely.
> They have healed the wound of my people lightly,
> saying, "Peace, peace,"
> when there is no peace.

> Jeremiah 6:13–14

There were violent confrontations with those who saw Jeremiah as a threat, a subversive element who must be put out of the way. He was hated, hounded, arrested, beaten and thrown into a cistern where he nearly died. Suffering, lonely and rejected, Jeremiah was a failure. He had brought into the open the truth of Israel's failure to be God's people and to live according to the covenant. He stood before them as the symbol of their failure, and they could not bear it.

Jeremiah's experience produced two positive and abiding results. The first was that amid the desolation he found personal intimacy with God. Throughout his prophecy there are passages of dialogue, often called the "Confessions of Jeremiah", where he wrestles in God's presence with his vocation and with the miseries and anguish of his life. These "Confessions" reveal a loving relationship of obedience and trust which had not appeared in the Old Testament before Jeremiah's time. This is not to say that no one had been related to God in such an intimate interchange before; but this is its earliest documentation. The failure, the bleak meaninglessness of his situation, became for Jeremiah the place for knowing God. It was his desert. A tenderness touched him there in his failure, a faithful love that made it possible, and necessary, to go on. As the prophet embodied Israel in its failure, so too he stood for Israel under the tender mercy of God:

> Is Ephraim still my dear son,
> a child in whom I delight?

As often as I turn my back on him
I still remember him;
and so my heart yearns for him,
I am filled with tenderness towards him.
This is the very word of the LORD.

Jeremiah 31:20, NEB

There are echoes of Hosea in this: "Jeremiah has pressed where his contemporaries would not readily go, to the pain of God, to a place where only Hosea had ventured before."[2]

The second positive consequence of Jeremiah's work has been mentioned already. He saw beyond the hopelessness, beyond the collapse and death of the present order of things, to a new act of God. Because human strength was played out and human resources had nothing further to offer, the salvation which was still promised must be a radically new thing, comparable to the creative act itself; it would indeed be a new creation in the core of the human person. As a corrupt and sinful heart had been the source of all the disobedience and chaos, so the re-created individual person, obedient from the heart, would be the only possible foundation for a new order of righteousness and a new covenant with God. There was no way forward except through a free and total forgiveness of sins, and Jeremiah pointed the way.

We can see it in this light, because we know more of the story, but it is doubtful whether Jeremiah himself could see any positive results from his career. He did not think he knew the answers, nor could he dwell complacently on any prospect of a happy ending; his identification with his failed people was far too real for that. He was the last person to think of himself as a spiritual pioneer. He did find union with God amid desolation and disaster, as his "Confessions" testify; he found it not because he was a specially original person but because all our failure is redeemed in Christ, and Jeremiah was caught up into the mystery of Christ although he lived centuries earlier. We can see it so, but Jeremiah was not recommending people to find God in such a way as that,

and it is unlikely that he saw his life as anything except
tragedy and total loss. As the nation collapsed into a sea of
agony, Jeremiah's death was probably as bleak and bitter as
most of his life had been. Like Judah, Jeremiah was losing
the lot.

There is another suffering figure in the prophetic tradition
who towers above Jeremiah and all the prophets in moral
stature, whose failure and death point more directly to the
death of Jesus than does anything else in the Old Testament.
He is the Servant of the Lord whose mission is described in
four songs embedded in the later parts of the Book of Isaiah.[3]
The Servant's portrait is probably composite; there are traits
of Jeremiah in him but perhaps royal features as well. He
transcends the bounds of any individual life and corresponds
to no historical figure known to us within the period covered
by the Old Testament. The overwhelming weight of
Christian tradition has seen these songs as a prophecy of the
ministry, passion and resurrection of Jesus Christ.

Any prophecy, however, had a relevance to its own day,
even though it had to wait for Christ before its full meaning
could be unfolded. The author of the songs was not simply
gazing into the future and singing of something unintelligible
to his contemporaries. Israel itself was called to be the Lord's
servant, and indeed explicitly given this title within the
prophecy where the songs occur. The Servant of the songs
stands in a complex relationship to Israel. At times he is
clearly God's messenger sent to the people, yet he is also in
some sense identified with Israel. He seems to be an
embodiment of the people – Israel fully realizing its vocation
– and at the same time to become more and more clearly
individualized as the songs proceed; he is someone who
preaches to the people and eventually dies for them.
Probably there was fluidity in the author's understanding, as
he came to see first that Israel as a whole was failing in its
vocation; then that even a remnant of Israel or a spiritual élite
would fail; then that some historical figure who seemed to be
a saviour (such as the Persian king Cyrus whose victories
occasioned Israel's return from Babylon) was inadequate too;

and finally that salvation could be effected only through an unknown individual Servant of the Lord who would come in the future.

When the Servant is introduced he seems to be a prophet chosen by the Lord and living in close intimacy with him. On him the Spirit of the Lord rests, and he is gentle and compassionate:

> He will not cry or lift up his voice
>   or make it heard in the street;
> a bruised reed he will not break,
>   and a dimly burning wick he will not quench.
>
> Isaiah 42:2–3

Yet for all the gentleness there is an impression of youth, vigour and high hopes. He has been called, like Jeremiah, from his mother's womb, and the Lord

> made my mouth like a sharp sword,
>   in the shadow of his hand he hid me;
> he made me a polished arrow,
>   in his quiver he hid me away.
>
> Isaiah 49:2

Wide horizons are open before him, for he is sent not only to bring back the tribes of Israel, but to be a light to all nations, the bearer of the Lord's salvation to the ends of the earth. He lives close to God, as a listener:

> The Lord GOD has given me
>   the tongue of those who are taught,
> that I may know how to sustain with a word
>   him that is weary.
> Morning by morning he wakens,
>   he wakens my ear,
>   to hear as those who are taught.
>
> Isaiah 50:4

Through the Servant God will win himself glory. So far it looks like the beginning of a successful mission.

Another note is sounded, however, as the Servant grows weary and discouraged:

> I said, "I have laboured in vain,
>   I have spent my strength for nothing and vanity."
>
>   Isaiah 49:4

In the third song he is confronting not merely unresponsive apathy but sharp opposition and physical violence:

> I gave my back to the smiters,
>   and my cheeks to those who pulled out the beard;
> I hid not my face
>   from shame and spitting.
> For the Lord GOD helps me;
>   therefore I have not been confounded;
> therefore I have set my face like a flint,
>   and I know that I shall not be put to shame.
>
>   Isaiah 50:6–7

This kind of conflict recalls Jeremiah, but by the fourth song the Servant's journey from success to failure seems complete: here is a failed, degraded prophet with no peer in the Old Testament; here is failure at its starkest and rawest:

> He had no form or comeliness that we should look at him,
>   and no beauty that we should desire him.
> He was despised and rejected by men;
>   a man of sorrows, and acquainted with grief.
>
>   Isaiah 53:2–3

The Servant is disfigured, bruised and wounded, evidently by his people. Yet he is also the living image of the people, as First Isaiah had seen it:

> Your head is covered with sores,
>   your body diseased;
> from head to foot there is not a sound spot in you –
> nothing but bruises and weals and raw wounds.
>
> Isaiah 1:5–6, NEB

And so from this unbearable sight "people screen their faces" (53:3), not simply because the Servant is loathsome and unsightly but because, standing leper-like before them, he images forth the truth about themselves. The ugliness is the living image of "*our* transgressions, *our* sins":

> On himself he bore our sufferings,
>   our torments he endured,
> while we counted him smitten by God,
>   struck down by disease and misery;
> but he was pierced for our transgressions,
>   tortured for our iniquities . . .
> We had all strayed like sheep,
>   each of us had gone his own way;
> but the LORD laid upon him
>   the guilt of us all.
>
> Isaiah 53:4–6, NEB

The ghastly devastation written on a contorted face and a tormented body is a sign for us, a visual aid to bring our sin into the open. The truth would be unbearable if the sign finished there, but there is a vision beyond it:

> The chastisement he bore is health for us
> and by his scourging we are healed.
>
> Isaiah 53:5, NEB

How such healing can be brought about is more than the Old Testament can say, but there are clues in the fourth song, positive perspectives that open towards another figure, the true Servant. The intimacy and trust in God already found in the earlier songs have matured into heroic obedience, for the Servant is not so much the helpless victim of violence as a willing, silent volunteer:

> He was oppressed, and he was afflicted,
>   yet he opened not his mouth;
> like a lamb that is led to the slaughter,
>   and like a sheep that before its shearers is dumb,
>   so he opened not his mouth.
>
> Isaiah 53:7

His death is a free self-offering that has the dignity, and more than the dignity, of ritual sacrifice, for "he makes himself an offering for sin". Cut off from life, with no stake in the future, no posterity to perpetuate his name and guarantee his survival, he yet

> shall see his offspring, he shall prolong his days . . . he shall see the fruit of the travail of his soul and be satisfied . . . Therefore I will divide him a portion with the great, and he shall divide the spoil with the strong.
>
> Isaiah 53:10–12

Throughout the agony, one thing has impelled him, love for his oppressors. For their healing he has interceded. Not until the coming of him who, though sinless, was "made sin for us" will the Scriptures see so deeply into the meaning of failure. It is beginning to be clear why failure was intrinsic to a prophet's vocation. He fails signally; the word is exact.

*

There is one more figure in this succession of God's failers at whom we must look before we turn to the one whose way they prepared. John the Baptist was a prophet and more than a prophet, and he stood at the hinge of history. He was Jesus's Public Relations Officer, responsible especially for first impressions.

Under the influence of the Spirit who had filled him even before his birth John sought the desert in a life of austerity, silence and prayer, uniting himself to the powerful tradition of his people, who in the desert had known God. He made himself marginal by his way of life, but as soon as he began to preach repentance he drew the crowds like a magnet. He was still a man set apart, still one of whom people could be frightened, whose uncompromising tongue and single-minded dedication awed them. But we are seeing only one side of John if we think of him as harsh, fierce and terrifying. The gospels leave us in no doubt that he was attractive. People flocked to him; he was popular. Even Herod Antipas, sensual and cruel, was fascinated by the light that was in John, the light of truth and purity that showed up Herod's vices:

> Herod was afraid of John, knowing him to be a good and holy man, and gave him his protection. When he had heard him speak he was greatly perplexed, and yet he liked to listen to him.
>
> Mark 6:20, JB

So did very many others. John was a great success. His followers were loyally attached to him, and he taught them to pray. Some people even believed him to be the Messiah, though he disclaimed it.

Then Jesus appeared, the man whose coming had been the whole reason for John's ministry. John pointed him out, and then stood aside watching his own disciples drop away from him to follow Jesus. He was content that they should:

> A man can have only what God gives him. You yourselves can testify that I said, "I am not the Messiah; I have been sent as his forerunner." It is the bridegroom to whom the bride belongs. The bridegroom's friend, who stands by and listens to him, is overjoyed at hearing the bridegroom's voice. This joy, this perfect joy, is now mine. As he grows greater, I must grow less.
>
> John 3:27–30, NEB

John is the patron saint of all who have been made redundant. His selfless shines out as perfect joy, and it is an invitation to every one of us, because redundancy is something we all have to learn at some time. His own light was waning as Christ the true light, the Sun of Righteousness, rose with healing in his rays. John allowed himself to become marginal in a different way now, and there was no glamour in it. Joy there was, but at what a cost in pain and bewilderment we may guess. He was like Moses, allowed to stand on the threshold of the promised land, but not to enter it. Perhaps John wondered why Jesus had not chosen him to be one of the apostles. Surely he was not unemployable? What was he to do now? With the ushering in of the kingdom he had preached he found himself without a job.

Apparently he went on doing what he could, but from the sidelines. He stood up for morality even when it involved confrontation with the great and powerful, and he was thrown into prison. There is great poignancy in the little we are told about the last stage of John's career. At one point he sent some of the disciples who were still in contact with him to ask Jesus, "Are you the one who is to come, or are we to expect some other?" (Matthew 11:3, NEB). Perhaps this was simply a means of informing the disciples who were sent; perhaps the question was put into John's mouth by the source from which the evangelist drew it in order to give Jesus the cue for his reply and the chance to point to the signs that accompanied his ministry. Such explanations are plausible enough, but the simplest and most obvious one is that John really wanted to know. At this late stage, after giving his life to his prophetic task with complete fidelity and finally enduring imprisonment, lonely and almost friendless, with little hope of release and at high risk of death, he wanted to know if his whole career had been a mistake. It was as bad as that.[4]

Heroically faithful and selfless, unsupported by any close companionship with Jesus, John died in squalid circumstances at the behest of a resentful princess.

The stem was pruned to enable the bud. John's redundancy was necessary to Jesus's success during the early part of his public life. It was the light of Jesus's popularity that eclipsed John. These facts suggest something of how John was trusted by Jesus, and by God. He was trusted enough to be assigned such a role, trusted to be a failure for the sake of Jesus.

4

The Failed Messiah

Gateways and thresholds are important. Human life is a journey, and our passage through a gateway from one stage of it to the next may be exciting, or joyful, or frightening, or painful and sad; but seldom is it an experience that leaves us indifferent. Most human societies have evolved "rites of passage", and even the modern West celebrates a coming of age, a housewarming, a graduation, an engagement or marriage, and retirement from one's job. A bride is still sometimes carried over the threshold of her new home. When people approach some very significant gateway in their lives, such as marriage or ordination to the priesthood, they may need to withdraw for a time into silence in order to pray and prepare themselves.

When Jesus came to the Jordan where John was baptizing he must have known that he was leaving behind the hidden years of peace and safety. A new stage was before him, the work for which all those years of quiet growth had been a preparation. Possibly he did not know beforehand why he came to John; he may simply have known that acceptance of John's baptism was the next step he must take, because his Father wanted it. The scene is full of meaning. Jesus humbly went down into the waters, which had been the sign of primeval chaos, as though he were rehearsing his descent into the dark, chaotic waters of death. As he came up the Father's voice was heard: "You are my beloved Son; in you I delight." The words combine a declaration of Messianic sonship with God's address to the Servant in the first Servant Song: Jesus is Son of David and Son of God, and he is also God's Servant. His emergence from the waters is a symbolic anticipation of his rising from the waters of death to the glory befitting his divine sonship. The Spirit rests on him as God's Wind (or Spirit, or Breath; the word is the same in Hebrew) had hovered over the watery chaos in the beginning, bringing life and beauty where there was nothing.

Jesus was intensely, passionately human, and this event must have been for him an experience of the utmost importance. Since childhood he had been learning to know the Father and grappling with the mystery of himself as the Father's Son, as depth beyond depth opened to his maturing mind. Human beings commonly learn by fits and starts; our growth in understanding seems to take a leap after a long period of consolidation, and possibly this experience at the Jordan was such a leap for Jesus. The love that had been addressing him all his life came home to him at a new depth. "You are my Son, and I love you." He had to withdraw for a while to come to terms with it. He needed time to think, time to pray. He went into the desert, to be alone with the Loved One. He needed that stripping of the spirit which comes from fasting and denying oneself comfort. The desert was his doorway, and Mark's gospel says that the Spirit "drove" him to it.

There was more than his personal need, however, in this decision for the desert. He was going back to the roots of his people's history, because he was of the flesh and blood of Israel. Like Elijah, Jesus went back to the beginnings, back to the place of formative experience and testing, back to the place of sin, bad memories and failure. As Hosea had suggested, this place of bad memories for Israel was about to become a door of hope.

There in the desert Israel had suffered and hungered, and Jesus too suffered and hungered, but opened himself to God's word, which is as necessary as bread to hungering human hearts. There Israel had rebelled and challenged God, and Jesus too was tempted to assert himself and challenge God, but chose instead to obey and trust his Father. There where false gods and empty promises had seduced Israel, Jesus too was tempted to seek power and glory for himself by idolatrous compromise, but chose instead to walk the way of service, worshipping his Father. In the desert where ancient memories and echoes were so powerful, he lived again his people's history; he made it his own but changed its meaning. He went freely into the place of weakness and failure and bad memories, but there he knew the Father and was known by him at a depth of intimacy and love unprecedented in human history. He must have listened and listened, there in the silence, to the word within him: "You are my Son; I love you." Temptation, struggle, austerity there were, with no distractions or human support to palliate them; but there must have been intense joy too.

His forty days echoed Israel's forty years, and when they were over he came back to Galilee "in the power of the Spirit" (Luke 4:14). His career was before him and he plunged into it with joy. He worked incredibly hard, shirking nothing. He taught the people as no one ever had before, and this must have taken no little thought and preparation, often at night when he was tired. He walked many miles in the heat and was jostled by crowds. He was endlessly available, even to people who intruded on what had been planned as a time of prayer or a weekend's rest. He was extremely popular, and he loved people. This is a costly lifestyle, and he invested in it all he had. He was obedient unto life for years before he became obedient unto death.

The people responded, sensing something radically new; through this intensely human personality something – Someone – more than human was touching them. They marvelled and praised him: "No one has ever spoken like this man . . . This teaching is new, with power behind it . . . He makes the deaf hear and the dumb speak . . . Lord, if you want to, you can cure me . . . " In their need they stretched out their hands to his human compassion, and touched the holiness of God. It was as though spring had broken loose among them after an age-long winter.

It was a time of amazing success, and amid it all Jesus was open to the Father, constantly seeking to plunge back into the current of love between them, praying, listening to the

Father's word, contriving times of silent communion with him. He was receiving life as sheer gift, and thanking the Giver. Success was to be celebrated together, with joy.

His obedience was demanding in the sense that any deeply loving relationship is demanding. It was a shared adventure of love. Jesus trusted his Father and knew that the Father completely trusted him. He was free within his obedience to live and laugh and grow and explore. His searching in prayer to know his Father and expose himself to this central love was not an anxious search for the right answers, as though obedience to the Father's will were something like looking for clues in a treasure hunt or a crossword puzzle. It was far more human and creative than that. He had to use all his intelligence to find out how to tackle any problem, to discern the best approach to people in each case, to find out how to translate his own experience of the Father into something they could grasp. He had to work hard at understanding people, opening his heart to different kinds of temperaments and different needs, trying to stay open when it hurt, studying how to help. It was not automatic for him any more than it is for us. Every individual mattered, and to each one Jesus was open, ready to learn and receive as well as to give, compassionate and humbly respectful. He tried to give each person room to be himself or herself, and clearly he succeeded, but at cost. Compassionate openness means vulnerability.

Jesus had to grapple with tensions, as every mature human being must, for maturity implies a capacity to live with tensions and allow them to be creative. In each of us there are the claims of body and spirit, the child and the adult, heart and head, male and female, *animus* and *anima*. The need to balance outgoing activity with the unity of inwardness confronts us all; we have to live with the competing claims of human sociability and solitude, the many and the one, aggressive effort and quiet acceptance, giving and receiving. A fully human life holds great forces together in the creative tension of love, and Jesus consented to be the still centre where these mighty tensions were reconciled. He was compassionate and tough, energetic and sensitive, brave and gentle, generous and receptive. He was the Servant who would not break a bruised reed or quench a dimly burning wick, but also the Servant who could set his face like flint.

We seldom feel that we have balanced our lives successfully in our attempt to reconcile these tensions, but it may help if we remember that life characteristically proceeds with a certain loss of balance. Here is a parable. A friend of mine runs a Day Centre once a week for elderly, handicapped and housebound adults. He collects them by car and they thoroughly enjoy it. When returning an elderly woman to her home at the end of a day he found himself standing in the road with his arms round her, helplessly stuck. He had succeeded in getting her out of his car but her legs were too rigid and she could not walk to the house. There they were, marooned and fixed, in a mixture of distress and laughter. Walking is a matter of losing one's balance again and again as the weight shifts first to one foot, then to the other. Excessive rigidity inhibits it. Similarly people who live life to the uttermost tend to be conscious of a loss of balance at times. It may be a genuine mistake, as happens when the shift of weight is so uncontrolled that we topple over instead of walking; but the imbalance may be part of a larger dance step.

Jesus must often have felt that he was losing his balance during those intensely lived days when the demands nearly overwhelmed him and it was difficult to find time to pray or eat or sleep. He must have felt at times that he was not getting it right; he was not immunized by his godhead against human mistakes and failures. One particularly painful failure was his rejection by his own people at Nazareth:

> They said, "Where did the man get all this? What is this wisdom that has been granted him, and these miracles that are worked through him? This is the carpenter, surely . . .?" And they would not accept him. And Jesus said to them, "A prophet is only despised in his own

country, among his own relatives and in his own house";
and he could work no miracle there . . . He was amazed
at their lack of faith.

Mark 6:2–6, JB

His very success scandalized them, and among his nearest
and dearest he failed. It must have been a bitter experience.
Perhaps there were other failures: a malaise about the wrong
kind of tension growing up between himself and Judas, and
his inability to penetrate the self-sufficiency of some who did
not know how much they needed him.

He had to keep letting go and trying again, abandoning
plans or methods that had proved inadequate, and giving up
visions that no longer corresponded to the truth he was
coming to see. His growth was a series of self-transcending
leaps as time after time he let go and trusted the Father at
some new turn in the road: "Father, into your hands I
commit my work, my hopes, my future, my tired body and
my spirit." He dared and explored, and allowed himself to
be stretched to the limits of what being human, and being
Son, meant. Life for him, and for those who shared it with
him, was joyful, humorous, loving, tender, demanding,
exasperating and rarely dull.

In all this activity Jesus learned humanly to know his
Father, but there were special moments when the people's
need for healing and his own compassion almost forced him
to a new level of trust and a new willingness to allow the
Father's love to go through him. When a blind man, or a
leper, or the mother of a sick child cried out to him in their
extremity, the anguish of sinful and wounded humanity
directly confronted the saving love of God incarnate in Jesus;
but we cannot believe that the healing he gave them was
automatic. Miracles are not magic, and though Jesus was Son
of God he did not operate simply by switching on divine
power. God works humanly in Jesus, and this means not only
through his eyes and hands and voice, but through his
psychological and spiritual humanity as well. The miracles
were hard work and made great demands on him. Early in

the ministry, as reported by the Synoptics, there is a series of events that gives us a little insight:

> A man appeared, covered with leprosy. Seeing Jesus he fell on his face and implored him. "Sir," he said, "if you want to, you can cure me." Jesus stretched out his hand, touched him and said, "Of course I want to! Be cured!" And the leprosy left him at once. He ordered him to tell no one, "But go and show yourself to the priest and make the offering for your healing as Moses prescribed it, as evidence for them."
>
> His reputation continued to grow, and large crowds would gather to hear him and have their sickness cured, but he would always go off to some place where he could be alone and pray.
>
> Luke 5:12–16, JB

The leper who appeared before Jesus was like a sign, an anguished individual in extreme need who stood for anguished humankind crying out to God. Jesus could not remain unmoved, because it touched him too nearly; it confronted him with the whole meaning of his mission. He had come to free men and women from the grip of evil, and here was the symbol of evil directly in his path, tormenting a human person. Most of us are capable of absent-mindedness in some degree; we can go about daily tasks and perform routine duties without explicitly adverting all the time to the deepest realities of our life, to the love of God that gives us meaning and to our bond with our fellow humans. When suddenly confronted with great love, or great suffering, or any situation which shocks us out of our ordinary mood, we find the deep things surfacing: we have to believe, or love, or trust, or consent to suffer in a very explicit and deliberate way. We affirm consciously and freely what is true all the time. Making all due allowances for the uniqueness of Jesus, we may suppose that something comparable happened to him. The encounter jolted him into explicit acceptance of his mission. His human compassion went out instinctively to the sufferer, but more than this was needed; Jesus had to allow the compassionate love of God to be incarnate in him. His human compassion was the place where the tender compassion of a healing, saving God met the anguish of wounded humanity, but only in the measure to which Jesus consented. He was like an open door, through which they could meet.

The demands it made on him were therefore very great. He had to be open to every human need, genuinely accessible and responsive. He had to enter into the place of pain, to "suffer together" with the person who cried to him, because this is what "compassion" means. And he had to be open to the Father, consenting to be ever more deeply the beloved Son in his manhood, in order to be the place of meeting for God and humankind. This meant obedience, trust, and letting go into the Father's hands in a new act of self-surrender. His human willingness to be the obedient Son was the crucial factor in the gift of healing.

Challenged by the cry for help, Jesus consented to do now, for this individual, what as Servant he was to do for the many by laying down his life. The healing act was a new creation, the ultimate new creation of the redeemed cosmos writ small and snatched early for the benefit of one suffering leper. In any truly creative action there is risk, because it is new and unprecedented. The leper took the risk of faith and leapt, abandoning respectable reticence, braving the reactions of bystanders who wanted him to keep his distance, and prepared to look a fool in public if his appeal failed. There were no cautious qualifications, no hedging of bets; he simply trusted Jesus. Jesus loved it, and responded, but not by any automatic application of power. He had to take a risk too, and be prepared to look a fool himself if it failed. He knew his Father's love would not fail him, but each time there was the new risk, the new leap, the new unknowing. Together he and the leper trusted, and together they stood in the stream of healing, because this very willingness to fail is an openness to God's love and healing and grace.

At this fine point where divine power touches human

beings through Jesus in the creative act, we wonder, "Could it have failed? Did God himself risk failure? *Does* he?" But for the present it succeeded, and the leper went free. God and a human sufferer rejoiced together. Jesus looked on what he had done and he rejoiced, for behold it was very good.

The price was paid not only in physical and psychological tiredness as the crowds besieged him demanding cures, but in the "suffering together" which his compassionate response implied; and so he habitually withdrew to pray. He needed prayer not simply to recruit his strength but to go to the roots of his mission, to grapple with the meaning of sickness and healing and enter more deeply into his vocation to be obedient Son and compassionate Servant. He needed prayer more and more as the demands multiplied, and he came to realize that the Father was asking of him a yet greater and more demanding work. Inner healing, the forgiveness of sins: this was his ultimate task, and it would cost his all. Like the suffering prophets but far more profoundly, he was consenting to be identified with his people and take their sins upon himself.

As his work proceeded Jesus was increasingly confronted by a need greater than that of lepers or paralytics or prostitutes, the need of those who were locked in hatred, self-sufficiency, pride, fear and hardness of heart. They were the apparently successful people, and they did not want him. They were in worse case than any others, because they were blind to their need and could not cry out. With them all his earlier approaches were bound to fail. As he set his face to go to Jerusalem, the prophet-killing city, for the last part of his ministry, he must have known it.

The death and raising of Lazarus, reported in graphic detail by John, are a sign of this far more difficult ministry to those hardened against Jesus. There are other raisings of dead people, reported more briefly by the Synoptics, but this one has special features. Lazarus is not merely dead; he has been dead for four days and is buried. Thus although Lazarus had been personally friendly to Jesus, he typifies a hopeless situation. Even his sisters, close friends of Jesus and believers in his power, can think only in terms of what might have been: "Lord, if you had been here, my brother would not have died" (John 11:21). But you were not here, and now it is too late.

Lazarus was locked in a tomb, unable even to cry out to Jesus for help as the lepers and blind and cripples had cried. He is a sign of our ultimate failure, the failure of death itself, that failure which would have locked us out for ever from the presence of the living God. To Jesus Lazarus must have been a terrible sign of those who had locked their own hearts against him. In this situation of ultimate hopelessness he confronted human need, and once again he allowed divine compassion to become incarnate in his own grief and longing:

> Jesus loved Lazarus . . . and he wept. So the Jews said, "See how he loved him!" . . . Then Jesus, deeply moved . . . came to the tomb.
>
> John 11:5, 35–36, 38

He surrendered into the Father's hands in a new maturity of trust. John emphasizes this. Jesus had been curiously slow when the news of Lazarus's illness was brought to him; he had wasted two precious days in spite of the urgency of the case. This was strange, for swift responses were characteristic of him; but now it almost looked as though he had taken care that he should arrive too late. Did he have to dawdle from some internal necessity, because it was part of his total reliance on the Father in this extremity, even as Gideon had whittled down his army, and Elijah had poured water over the offerings on Carmel until they were drenched, to make the fire miracle more "difficult"? It may have been thus between the Father and the incarnate Son at this moment of stretching and risk; Jesus was refusing even to take sensible measures to secure things humanly, because he knew that this event was crucial. He called his friends to join him in his surrender:

I am the resurrection . . . Do you believe this? . . . Have
I not told you that if you believe you will see the glory of
God?

John 11:25, 26, 40, JB

Lazarus, the sign of our sin and our hopeless failure, heard
the voice of the Son of God, "Lazarus, come forth!" Come
forth, sinful humankind, from the death of your spirits even
now by believing in me, and from the death of your flesh in
the end, because I am the resurrection. The place of
hopelessness, the place of death which is your last failure, has
become the place for seeing the glory of God.

The glory was seen, but the story is already pointing to the
means by which Jesus would reach those who were hardened
against him. The scene at Lazarus's raising anticipates many
traits of Easter: the mourning women at the tomb, the grave-
clothes, the rolling away of the stone, Jesus's distress and his
demand for faith. The miracle stands in a direct relation to
his own death in that it precipitated the decision of Caiaphas
and the chief priests and Pharisees to kill him; but the events
were linked inwardly as well. He would not be content to
stand outside a tomb, calling into it; his only way to reach
the impenitent was to go with them into their place of lonely,
meaningless death, and make that very place of Godforsaken
hopelessness the place of openness to God. He could
transform their failure only by failing himself.

Nevertheless he was still a free man after raising Lazarus,
and he could have escaped. Even in these dangerous last
weeks of the ministry he could have gone into hiding and lain
low until the trouble died down. It would still have been
possible to flee as Judas and the soldiers approached
Gethsemane, but he chose not to. There are occasions in our
lives when failure, suffering and humiliation can be avoided,
but only at the price of infidelity to God. Jesus stayed, and
nearly broke down in the garden. He was a thoroughly sane
and courageous man, with all the ability of a mature adult to
endure strain; but he could crack. He would not have been
human otherwise.

The cross is the passive fulfilment of all the strong activity of his ministry; it is the failure in view of which all the successful work had been possible. Only by embracing our failure at its starkest could Jesus heal all that failure, particularly the failure that masquerades as self-sufficiency and success. He went willingly to the cross, but in unimaginable darkness of spirit, weakness and fear. The solitude of Calvary was a deeper solitude than the desert had been. These two solitudes, desert and Calvary, mark the beginning and end of his public career, but they are not alike. The desert had been the place of remembered failure, but Jesus had conquered there. On Calvary to all human appearances he finally failed. In the desert he had known the closeness of his Father as he pledged himself to obedience, but on Calvary he experienced abandonment, even, as it seemed, by the Father who loved him.

All the stretching of body and mind during his ministry culminated in the terrible stretching of the cross, with the cracking of muscles and pull on the hands. All the tensions with which he had bravely and joyfully grappled met in the tension of the two-way pull as he was hoisted between earth and heaven, his heart still struggling to be all for the mysterious Father and all for the people who needed him. The openness for which he had intelligently and lovingly worked was consummated in the passive endurance of being opened, in hands and feet and heart.

Beside him hung two other failures, thieves with whom the law had caught up at last. One of them was hardened, closed and abusive. The other, amid the squalor and degradation of his failing life, was open. "Jesus, remember me . . ." This man is the patron saint of any one of us who thinks it is too late, anyone who has ever listened to the lie that we have only one chance. He must have had chances without number, and wasted them all except the last. Hanging there in the agony of his failure, he found himself not alone.

Yet even to the closed-minded Jesus was still open; surely to his other fellow criminal, and explicitly to the torturers for whom he pleaded: "Father, forgive them; for they know not what they do" (Luke 23:34). His arms were stretched in a would-be embrace for all the world; his heart was laid open, the Lover's heart, the open door through which God's love and human need could meet.

Down the ages Christian theologians and mystics have asked why the cross was necessary. Simple believers (among whom theologians and mystics are also commonly numbered) have pondered the question and found no complete answer, though their intuition may come nearer to it than their logic when they know their own suffering to be in some way linked with Christ's. In the wilderness of Calvary a failed Messiah, hanging abandoned by nearly all his followers, made sense of all our unmeaning and all our failure. God has dealt with them by coming to join us there.

In his brokenness, Jesus became the place where our humanity was laid open to God. The Scriptures commonly speak of "flesh" as the antithesis of "spirit". "Flesh" means not the material component of human nature as such, but the whole human person, mind as well as body, in so far as we are closed against God. "Flesh" therefore stands for the false self-sufficiency of proud, disobedient humankind, closed in on itself and barred against love. In this sense "flesh" is the barrier to God's gift of his Holy Spirit, a barrier which had to be broken through. Jesus had identified with alienated humanity in all the conditions to which flesh had reduced it, including weakness, pain, failure and death; but by making these very conditions the means of his loving, obedient openness to the Father he had changed their whole significance. He died "in the likeness of sinful flesh" (Romans 8:3), but he died into his Father's hands, and his death was a breakthrough, a passover. The barriers were down between Lover and beloved. The Easter Christ is for ever an open channel for God's giving to the world, the place where the Spirit is freely given and freely received.

Freely received, because in his dying Jesus consummated his own human growth as loved Son. All his life had been a process of translating the glory of being the Father's eternal

Son into human terms. His trust, prayer, openness and joyful obedience were the human face of what that glory is within the Trinity, where the Father's delight is to give his all to the Son, and the Son's delight is to hold his godhead as sheer gift, giving himself back to the Father in the dance and embrace of eternal love. The Spirit is their kiss, the joy of their embrace, the movement of their dance, the infinite gift that unites them. When the Son became man he "learned obedience"; that is, he learned through life, love, human relationships and prayer to express in a human way the reality of being Son. In the Spirit he said "Father" throughout his unfolding life, but in a special way he learned obedience through suffering. When on the cross he said, "Father, into your hands I commit my spirit", he said "Father" as he had never said it before, from a new place in his experience, with overtones of love and obedience and self-giving of which he would not have been capable before that moment. It came from a deeper place than the agonized shout, "Why . . .?", a place of tenderness where he had never been before. The Father had longed and longed to hear "Abba" like that, from a human heart and human lips. In the psalms it had been predicted in the Lord's name, "He will say to me: 'You are my father'" (Psalm 88(89):27, Grail); the reference was to a son of David who would also be adopted son of the Lord. Many an of heir of David may have said "Father" to God, but none had ever said it like this. Human parents long to hear their child say "Daddy" or "Mummy", and their joy is a faint reflection of something in the heart of God.

The Word was made failure and died among us, but we saw his glory, glory as of the only-begotten Son of the Father. In his brokenness, in his overleaping failure, we see the glory, because God's glory is not power closed in on itself but the endless openness of self-surrendering love. Freely receiving in his manhood the Father's infinite gift of the Spirit, Jesus is free to give to all of us the Spirit who makes us children of God, the Spirit in whom we too say, "Abba", with the voice of children and heirs. The broken and glorified

Easter Christ releases for us the Spirit who operates from
within the deepest springs of human freedom, the Spirit who
alone can open us to one another and to God.

> Two trees
> proclaim in spring
> a word to the world
>
> one exploding
> into blossom
> trumpets glory
>
> one stretching
> dead limbs
> holds the empty
> body of God
>
> both speak
> with due reserve
> into the listening
> ear of the world.[1]

These two trees are like life and death, success and failure,
in the experience of each one of us, as in that of Jesus. Both
speak the word of God to us as they did to him. We know
and are known by God in our strength and our weakness. In
the preceding pages a contrast has been sketched between the
two phases of Jesus's ministry: the earlier one in Galilee when
he was on the whole successful, and the later one in
Jerusalem which he consummated by failure. There is a
difference; but the two are linked, especially by obedience.
There was no cult of failure in Jesus's life, and there should
be none in ours. He rejoiced in his strength and intelligence
and used them to the full; he tried his utmost to succeed. So
must we. Obedience was the dynamism of his life
throughout. Whether it led him into obviously fruitful work

or into invisibly fruitful failure, the Father's will was his single, all-embracing love.

Another unifying bond between the two periods of ministry was his compassionate love. Most of us have met in at least one other person an availability, an open hospitality of mind and heart which knows how to create a friendly space for anyone who comes, especially for the stranger, the frightened or suffering, the wounded or insecure. Such an attitude of compassionate openness grows from deep humility, from a genuine poverty of spirit and personal emptiness. If we lack this inner poverty we cannot create a friendly space for everyone; we will tend to be selective because we are mentally dismissing those from whom we do not think we have anything to learn. Or we may be subtly using others because we want to feel, and to be thought, kind and compassionate. In either case the other person will not have room to be himself or herself. Jesus must have discovered this too. The exigencies of his mission to every man, woman and child, as well as his obedient filial relationship to the Father, continually required him to grow in personal emptiness and poverty of spirit. Possibly the final shape of the saying recorded in Matthew 11:27–30 is no accident. In order to be able to say, "Come to me, all who labour and are heavy laden . . .", and allow his invitation to be accepted, he had to be meek and humble, lowly and poor in heart, or they would not have found rest and space unto their souls. But this poverty and emptiness, and this all-welcoming compassion, were possible for him only in the measure that he "knew" the Father as Son, and was "known" by the Father, because these qualities are Godlike. God never overwhelms us, or crushes, or disdains; he always has use for the little we bring and always knows us at our best. God is gentle and hospitable and welcoming, and his humility quietens our fear. We have space to grow and to be ourselves; we can speak our minds, be at home with him, and play.

On Easter Day the Roman liturgy plays with some verses of Psalm 139(138) in the Entrance Song at Mass. The risen

Christ is speaking to his Father: "I am risen and I am still with you . . . You laid your hand upon me . . . Wonderful is your knowing of me . . ." For the Hebrews "knowing" meant intimacy and surrender. In our measure we too can allow God to know us as we fail and suffer, because in that dark place we find ourselves not alone.

In Istanbul there is a fourteenth-century ikon of Christ's resurrection, which is represented, as often in Byzantine art, as "The Harrowing of Hell". A strong, virile Christ in the centre appears almost to be dancing, so rhythmic is the painting. With his outstretched right hand he grasps Adam's wrist and with his left Eve's, as he pulls them out of their graves. Their hands are weak and limp but Christ has them in a firm grip, and they scramble up in his strength to join him in his dance of life. Any failure and any suffering can be the place where he grasps us too, and draws us from our little hell into his open relationship to the Father and to all the others in the dance:

> O Lord, you search me and you know me,
> you know my resting and my rising . . .
> Behind and before you besiege me,
> your hand ever laid upon me . . .
> O where can I go from your spirit,
> or where can I flee from your face?
> If I climb the heavens you are there.
> If I lie in the grave, you are there.
> If I take the wings of the dawn
> and dwell at the sea's furthest end,
> even there your hand would lead me,
> your right hand would hold me fast.
>
> Psalm 138(139):1, 2, 5, 7–10, Grail

Christ has gone down into the deepest places of our failure and claimed them as his own, and now there is no possible failure in our lives or our deaths that cannot be the place of meeting him and so of greater openness to his work. Nevertheless real openness to God in failure and suffering is not to be identified too readily with a stiff upper lip. What passes for courage or obedience to God's will may be partly insensitivity or lack of imagination, and some pride may lurk under stoicism. This is delicate. Jesus himself did not run cheerfully along under his cross; he was weak and agonized and apparently needed help. A sound Christian instinct has included three falls in the devotional Stations of the Cross, though Scripture does not say he fell. Much of our life is spent in weakly stumbling on, falling and getting up again, and helping one another to get up. Most of our failures are unheroic and unglamorous. God loves us as we suffer weakly, despising ourselves, with no room for pride; he loves us because he cannot see us apart from his Son. We may in reality be more open amid the dark, bitter, meaningless chaos, more open to the utterly mysterious God. These moments may be the Lover's gateway. Yet we must still refuse self-pity and try not to make heavier weather of our failure than is necessary. God does not require us to cultivate it in order to do his work.

Failure or disappointment may be God's chance to open us more effectively than we can ever open ourselves, and to stretch us beyond our small hopes and expectations. This is the theme of the story in chapter 24 of Luke's gospel about the two disciples walking to Emmaus. They are dazed and stunned. The failure of Jesus is the failure of all their own plans, because "We had hoped that he was the one to redeem Israel" (Luke 24:21). A successful Jesus had raised their hopes and inspired them and won their love, but a failed and crucified Messiah left them shattered. The risen Jesus, patient and tender, walks with them, trying to make them understand, opening their minds to the Scriptures, stretching them, sharing his own Easter mind with them: Was it not written? Was it not necessary that Christ should suffer all this, and so enter into his glory?

These two travellers are you and I; they are the Church walking with Christ the long road of history. To us as to them he says, "Let go of your own plans. Your failure and disappointment are part of something larger, because your

Father's love for you is greater than you have begun to imagine. You fail for the same reason that I did; come into my Easter."

> Christ leads me through no darker rooms
> than he went through before;
> he that unto God's kingdom comes,
> must enter by this door . . .
>
> My knowledge of that life is small,
> the eye of faith is dim;
> but 'tis enough that Christ knows all,
> and I shall be with him.[2]

5

Let Him Easter

The two trees of the poem reproduced in chapter 4 grow in the life of every disciple, as they did in the mortal life of Jesus. Everyone who belongs to him rejoices at times in abundant life, and yet consents to many a little death. Each of us is called to know God and be known by him in our strength and success, which are his gift, and in our weakness and failure, where we need his compassion. Christ lives in the Church, which means in the lives of men and women. Both kinds of experience are a share in his ministry; in both he continues his redeeming work.

From the time when the Church was born of Christ's Easter death and resurrection, this double character has been stamped on every fully Christian life. It is not always a case of alternation between success and failure, life and death, strength and weakness; more often they interpenetrate. This is already evident in the New Testament, particularly in the lives of those who stood close to Jesus. With a few of them the present chapter is concerned.

Peter is a vividly human person, who muddles through the pages of the gospels with a consistent inconsistency that is entirely credible. His name, derived not from any wishful thinking on the part of his parents when he was too young to belie their expectations, but from Jesus's choice, is a name of strength, "the Rock". The Lord himself was often so called in the Old Testament. Yet this Rock-Man, Peter, is glaringly weak. When he encounters God in Jesus of Nazareth the close relationship between them reveals Peter's weakness in a series of failures, but through them he learns the essential lessons. He remains open to God's love throughout, and is made fit for a ministry in the Kingdom somewhat different from the role he might have designed for himself, a ministry best exercised by a man who has known failure and weakness at first hand.

Mark, Matthew and John place the call of Peter at the beginning of Jesus's public ministry. John's account is especially vivid: Andrew, Simon's brother, has been called first, and then,

> He found his brother Simon, and said to him, "We have found the Messiah" (which means Christ). He brought him to Jesus. Jesus looked at him, and said, "So you are Simon the son of John? You shall be called Cephas" (which means Peter).
>
> John 1:41–42

Peter was to have cause to remember that long, hard look of Jesus. He would meet it again at significant moments.

Luke, for his own reasons, places the call of Peter and the other apostles a little later, after Jesus has preached and worked a number of miracles. Peter's ready response is thus more understandable, but Luke also gives the call a special setting, associating it with an enormous catch of fish. Peter (or Simon, as he is called in the first part of Luke's story) was a professional fisherman, probably with a lifetime's experience. Nevertheless he had had a bad night, a night of failure, when Jesus passed by and wanted to use his boat as a convenient pulpit. When Jesus had finished speaking

> he said to Simon, "Put out into the deep and let down your nets for a catch." And Simon answered, "Master, we toiled all night and took nothing! But at your word I will let down the nets." And when they had done this, they enclosed a great shoal of fish; and as their nets were breaking, they beckoned to their partners in the other boat to come and help them. And they came and filled both the boats, so that they began to sink. But when Simon Peter saw it, he fell down at Jesus's knees, saying, "Depart from me, for I am a sinful man, O Lord." For he was

astonished, and all that were with him, at the catch of fish
which they had taken . . . And Jesus said to Simon, "Do
not be afraid; henceforth you will be catching men." And
when they had brought their boats to land, they left
everything and followed him.

Luke 5:4–11

After a night of failure, Peter came to know Jesus. Trusting
Jesus, he had an amazing success which Luke presents as a
prophetic sign of Peter's future ministry. Jesus met Peter on
a beach, the threshold between the firm, safe land and the
mysterious, unpredictable sea. Peter was used to crossing
this threshold, and he launched out readily into the watery
deep; but then he faced another deep, and knew himself to
be in the presence of the Holy One. The abundance of God's
gift overwhelmed him, and like Isaiah he cried out in his
sinfulness. Happily Jesus did not take literally the request,
"Depart from me"; he knew Peter, who was probably
clinging to him even as he spoke.[1]

During the next two or three years Peter was constantly
close to Jesus and trusted by him in a singular degree, but
he often failed to understand. He listened to Jesus speaking
of forgiveness, and made what he must have thought an
extravagantly generous proposal: "Lord, how often am I to
forgive my brother if he goes on wronging me? As many as
seven times?" After all, seven was the perfect number for the
Jews, so that would be perfection, surely? No, replied Jesus,
"Seventy times seven" (Matthew 18:21–22, NEB).
Nevertheless, Peter was a man with good eyes, and he had
moments of God-given insight. Through the earlier part of
the ministry Jesus taught and trained the apostles, bringing
them gradually to the point where they could make a
definitive act of faith in him. When the moment came it was
Peter who made the leap of faith and articulated his
conviction in the name of them all, and Jesus commended
him for his response to grace:

"Who do men say that the Son of Man is? . . . But who

do you say that I am?" Simon Peter replied, "You are the Christ, the Son of the living God." And Jesus answered him, "Blessed are you, Simon Bar-Jona! For flesh and blood has not revealed this to you, but my Father who is in heaven. And I tell you, you are Peter, and on this rock I will build my church, and the powers of death shall not prevail against it. I will give you the keys of the kingdom of heaven."

Matthew 16:13, 15–19

Jesus had known Peter truly. The rock-name he had given him earlier now seemed justified, for Peter had shown himself to be a man of faith. He who had been searched by Jesus's penetrating gaze had now seen with spiritual penetration himself; he had seen this carpenter, his friend, as he really was. He had recognized the unlikely Messiah; he had eyes for the upside-downness of God's world. He had risen to the heights of faith and grace. And immediately he fell from them, and failed once more.

Jesus foretold his passion, and Peter, perhaps still dreaming of the Kingdom of which he was to be key-bearer, saw fit to take him to task: "Heaven forbid!" he said. "No, Lord, this shall never happen to you." Jesus's reaction was swift and fierce: "Away with you, Satan; you are a stumbling-block to me. You think as men think, not as God thinks" (Matthew 16:22–23, NEB). It is the desert temptation over again, the proffer of an easy way to glory by selfish assertion of power and refusal of suffering; Jesus had rejected it then and rejected it again now, as we all have to do repeatedly even after dedicating ourselves to obedient discipleship. There are other echoes awakening too, echoes of the false prophets in Jeremiah's time who "healed the wound of [the] people lightly, saying, 'Peace, peace', when there is no peace" (Jeremiah 6:14). Peter was playing the false prophet: everything was going to be all right, there was no need to talk of suffering and death. Jesus confronted him as sharply as Jeremiah had clashed with the false prophets of his day. Jesus was never soft with Peter; he loved him too much. But he always gave him another chance.

This time the new chance seems to have followed quickly on the failure. Jesus took Peter, together with James and John, up a mountain where they could be alone to pray. It may have been at night, and something happened between Jesus and God which could not be put into human words, though imagery from the Old Testament is used by the evangelists to describe it. Jesus

> was transfigured before them, and his face shone like the sun, and his garments became white as light. And behold, there appeared to them Moses and Elijah, talking with him . . . and lo, a bright cloud overshadowed them, and a voice from the cloud said, "This is my beloved Son, with whom I am well pleased; listen to him."
>
> Matthew 17:2–5

Moses and Elijah, the two great men who had known something of the glory of the God of Israel on a mountain, were now receiving the fulfilment of their longing in a vision of Jesus. The cloud, which had been the sign of God's presence and holiness on Sinai, in the desert and in the temple, was present again. The Father's voice once more attested Jesus as the beloved Son, as at his baptism, and again with the nuance that he is also the Servant. The three trembling disciples saw and heard all this; how much was interior mystical experience and how much an event that they perceived with their senses we cannot determine, but they knew they were in the presence of God, and fell flat on their faces. Once more it was Peter who spoke while the others were silent, and once more he showed that his eyes had penetrated the earthly camouflage of Jesus and seen him as he really was. Yet Peter's contributions were a little wild; perhaps he felt he had to say something, but "he did not know what to say, for they were exceedingly afraid" (Mark 9:6). He rushed in with suggestions about building booths, probably with reference to the Jewish custom at the Feast of Tabernacles. It was inappropriate; but it did not matter. "Jesus came and touched them, saying, 'Rise, and have no fear.' And when they lifted up their eyes, they saw no one but Jesus only" (Matthew 17:7–8).

Even at the Last Supper Peter did not understand what Jesus was doing when, in an action which symbolized his identity as the humble Servant, he proposed to wash his disciples' feet. Probably none of the others did either, but it was typical of Peter first to blurt out his objections and then to capitulate wholeheartedly when he grasped that it was something to do with "having a part with" Jesus. He loved Jesus, but was still not fully attuned to his mind. A little later in the garden, when Jesus took the three privileged witnesses of the Transfiguration apart, to give him support in his agony by their loving though uncomprehending presence, Peter and the others fell asleep. They were sleeping for sorrow, says Luke (22:45), worn out by grief. Neither Peter nor the others had yet found room for the truth of a suffering and failing Messiah.

Nevertheless Jesus's assessment of Peter had not been mistaken. He had seen through the bravado and the confusions and known Peter as he truly was, great but weak. God sees us all as potentially transfigured in his beloved Son. Jesus never ceased to believe in Peter and to love him towards his true greatness, knowing what the experiences and compassion of this failing disciple would later mean to other weak and failing disciples. At the Last Supper Jesus had hinted at this: "Simon, Simon, beware: Satan demanded to have you all, to sift you like wheat. But for you, Simon, I have prayed that your faith may not fail; and once you have come back, you must strengthen your brothers" (Luke 22:31–32). Yet Peter had still not understood his need to draw on the Lord's strength. Trusting in his own, he had made the bold claim that even if all the rest should fall away, he would go with his Master to prison and death, whereupon Jesus had foretold Peter's greatest failure: before the cock had crowed twice, the Rock-Man would have disclaimed three times that he even knew him.

The prediction was verified a few hours later as Peter,

standing near the fire in the high priest's courtyard, frightened and hemmed in by hostile and suspicious servants, made his threefold denial. "At that instant, while he was still speaking, the cock crew, and the Lord turned and looked straight at Peter, and Peter remembered what the Lord had said to him . . . And he went outside and wept bitterly" (Luke 22:61–62, JB). The verb "looked straight at" is the same in Greek as that used in John's gospel of Jesus's hard, penetrating look at Peter at the time of his vocation. As Jesus had then seen Peter in his potential greatness and goodness, so now he saw him in his sin and failure, and Peter knew it.

That might have been the end, for a failure like this can be shattering. Peter might have rationalized and found plausible excuses for his night of failure; he might have argued that Jesus's cause was now hopeless in any case, that he himself was powerless to help any further, that it was Jesus's own express wish that his followers should go free. He did none of these things; he simply repented in all the humility and grief of which he was capable, and it broke him open, though for the next day or two he must have felt simply broken, with no "open" about it.

He is mentioned in several of the reports of the resurrection appearances, but most prominently in chapter 21 of John's gospel. Again the echoes awaken. There was a night of failure and fruitless work, during which skilled fishermen caught nothing, and then a knowing of the Lord. Another enormous catch of fish followed, and Jesus made of it a sign of Peter's ministry, but there was a personal matter to be settled between them first. Jesus seemed to be setting the scene deliberately: early morning, and a fire, as at the denial; a threefold question recalling the threefold disclaimer, which is now blotted out by a threefold declaration of love. Jesus is taking Peter back to the place of bad memories, the place where he failed, and transforming it. They meet on a beach, a threshold between land and sea and a threshold of vital importance in Peter's life. All that he lost is given back to him, and more. He is not simply forgiven; the care of all those whom Christ loves is entrusted to him. Only one qualification is required for the office, love. In this moment of forgiveness Peter can look again into the eyes that turned to him after his sin. He can bear to be known, because it is only love that he finds there, and in his new truth and humility he can say, "Lord, you know everything; you know I love you." He has entered deeply into the mystery of failure, and in it he has known God. He is therefore qualified at last to share the ministry of the failed Messiah and be himself the keeper of the gateway between heaven and earth. The new community will be a place where people fail and are forgiven.

We hear a good deal more of Peter after this threshold-time in his life; clearly it was not a case of living happily ever after. He faced great responsibility and momentous decisions, especially with regard to the admission of the gentiles into the new-born Church. He hesitated and no doubt made mistakes, but one episode recorded in the Acts of the Apostles is particularly suggestive of the transformation Christ had wrought in Peter. It occurs early, apparently soon after Pentecost, when the Christian community had not yet broken with Judaism and its members still frequented the temple for prayer. Peter and John went there one day and passed a cripple at the gate, a man accustomed to beg from all who went in. When he accosted them,

> Peter fixed his eyes on him, as John did also, and said, "Look at us." Expecting a gift from them, the man was all attention. And Peter said, "I have no silver or gold; but what I have I give you: in the name of Jesus Christ of Nazareth, walk." Then he grasped him by the right hand and pulled him up; and at once his feet and ankles grew strong; he sprang up, stood on his feet and started to walk. He entered the temple with them, leaping and praising God as he went.
>
> Acts 3:4–8, NEB

This is the first miracle Peter is reported to have worked, and surely it was for him, as for Jesus himself during his mortal life, an occasion of risk and faith, when he was invited to let himself go trustingly into the Father's hands. The Father did not fail him. No word of explicit faith is recorded from the lame man, but the command, "Look at us", is striking. Peter knew a good deal about communication through the meeting of eyes, and it may be that he invited the cripple to faith in the very way which had been so significant for himself. Like Jesus, he also used his hands. The vivid phrase, "grasped him by the right hand and pulled him up", recalls the strong Christ of the Byzantine ikon pulling Adam up from his grave, and Jesus grasping Peter as he sank in a stormy sea. Then Peter and John enter the temple with their joyful, healed companion, whose exuberance evokes the Messianic prophecy, "Then shall the lame men leap like a hart". Peter has been successful, because he lives and works "in the name of Jesus Christ of Nazareth", to whom he will be perfectly conformed in his death, when he "will stretch out his arms, and a stranger will bind him, and carry him where he has no wish to go" (cf. John 21:18).

Throughout these stories, Peter is someone with whom we instinctively identify because he is so ambiguous. He veers from insight to obtuseness and back again. In the long run he is the man whose failures are fruitful, because they draw him into the heart of Christ's Easter mystery; but from time to time he is to be found in the wrong camp. He is the great apostle, yet he plays the part of a false prophet; he typifies those who rely on their own strength, yet also those who in repentance are open to God's forgiveness. We recognize this, we who often find ourselves mirrored in contrasting groups in the gospels: in Martha *and* Mary, the prodigal *and* the elder son, the Pharisee *and* the tax collector, the good soil which welcomes the seed *and* the thorny soil which stifles it. The divisions are within ourselves.

Peter was one of Christ's successes. It seems that Judas was one of his failures. So the New Testament presents it, though we cannot know what passed between Judas and God at the end. "'Twixt the stirrup and the ground there's mercy

sought and mercy found", as the proverb has it, so there was
time for Judas to seek and find between the jump and the
tightening of the noose. Nevertheless the sources leave his
memory a dark enigma, without even suggesting a motive for
his treachery other than greed. Some people have thought
this inadequate and suggested that he was proud, a perverted
idealist, a man who tried to manipulate Jesus and then
dropped him when he refused to comply. There may be truth
in these theories but we have no means of knowing. What is
clear is that he closed his heart. His sin was no more
unforgivable than Peter's; only his refusal to open himself to
God made the difference.

Early in his narrative of the public life, John says of Jesus,

many gave their allegiance to him when they saw the signs
that he performed. But Jesus for his part would not trust
himself to them. He knew men so well, all of them, that
he needed no evidence from others about a man, for he
himself could tell what was in a man.

John 2:23–25, NEB

This is obviously true of Jesus's divine knowledge, but his
divinity did not cramp his manhood. Part of being human is
that we are ignorant and make mistakes, not only in trifling
matters where they can be easily rectified but in great
decisions where our mistakes can have far-reaching
consequences. Jesus was not protected by his godhead
against this possibility, and although he was highly
intelligent and shrewd, with a clear gaze that usually
penetrated to the core of every person he met, he was capable
of making mistakes, and it looks as though he did make one
in choosing Judas. Yet perhaps to put it like this distorts the
mysterious truth. Jesus did know Judas in his potential
sainthood, as he also knew Peter; he called Judas and loved
and trusted him, but Judas was still free. Something went
wrong between them, and Jesus had to live with his choice,
and eventually die with it. All this was for him part of the
obedience, the trust, the risk of being human; it had terrible

consequences but was directly taken up into his Easter. The same is true of our mistakes.

Judas's decision to betray him cannot have been sudden. There must have been a progressive estrangement and infidelity, of which his overt treachery was the logical climax, and Jesus was too sensitive not to have been aware of it. He must have tried and tried again with Judas, praying and thinking and searching for the way to get through to him, longing to get past the fear or pride or resentment or whatever block it was, to touch the core of goodness in Judas and reawaken love. And he failed. It must have been one of the most bitter of his failures; its poignancy is suggested by a phrase in the prayer after the Last Supper which John attributes to him. Speaking to the Father, Jesus says,

> I have manifested thy name to the men whom thou gavest me out of the world; thine they were, and thou gavest them to me . . . While I was with them I kept them in thy name . . .; I have guarded them, and none of them is lost but the son of perdition.
>
> John 17:6, 12

These loved men were the Father's gift to him, a precious, entrusted gift; and he has lost none of them – except Judas. He has failed with Judas. In his anguish is the anguish of parents who mourn over a child, God's gift to them, who has gone wrong. In his failure is the failure of any one of us who has tried to help someone who in the end refuses. A consultant psychiatrist who was once invited to address an important scientific convention chose to read a paper on his failures, on those of his patients whom he had failed to reach, who had committed suicide. In a less professional form most of us have had some comparable experience. Christ has known this place of our failure.

*

Peter is an outstanding example of a person who shared both the successful ministry of Jesus and his ministry of failure.

The New Testament provides another: Paul.

It is usual to think of Paul as an instance of dramatic conversion, one who represents in an extraordinary way the U-turns that can occur in our lives. There is truth in this, but it must not be understood simplistically, because there is evidence both of preparation before God brought him to the moment of conversion on the Damascus road, and of consolidation after it. His life was as much a mixture of success and failure as Peter's, though his temperament, character, circumstances and vocation were vastly different.

Paul had been a successful Pharisee, with all this entailed of hard study under Gamaliel, of effort, self-discipline and zeal. As far as was humanly possible he had successfully kept the Law. All his energy and single-minded concentration, all his search to know God in the revelation given to Israel, culminated in his determination to crush the new religion which had sprung from Jesus of Nazareth, for he was too intelligent to think it simply harmless. He must have known intuitively from the first that the Gospel of salvation in Christ radically contradicted his own passionate belief in salvation through the keeping of the Law. He had gone as far as anyone could go in self-perfection, and by legal reckoning his life was a success. Then he was struck down.

However dramatic, it was not simply a bolt from the blue; that Christ had in some way been in touch with Paul before this day is suggested by the words, "Saul, Saul, why do you persecute me? It hurts you to kick against the goads" (Acts 26:14). He had felt the goads, evidently, and Stephen's Christlike death must have impressed him; but now he surrendered, gave himself in faith and love to the risen Christ who had appeared to him, and accepted baptism. From his own account in Galatians 1:17 it seems that soon afterwards he went to the desert. He must have needed solitude and prayer to re-orientate his life and his mind, to consolidate and adjust after the experience which had put Christ at the centre of his life. It is hard to admit that one has made a mistake, harder still to admit that one's whole life has been misdirected. It may be a very painful process to turn things upside-down, or it may be joyful, or both; but in any case it takes time.

By the time he wrote to the Philippians he could look on all he had formerly gained as well lost for love:

> If anyone thinks to base his claims on externals, I could make a stronger case for myself; circumcised on the eighth day, Israelite by race . . . a Hebrew born and bred; in my attitude to the law, a Pharisee; in pious zeal, a persecutor of the church; in legal rectitude, faultless. But all such assets I have written off because of Christ. I would say more: I count everything sheer loss, because all is far outweighed by the gain of knowing Christ Jesus my Lord, for whose sake I did in fact lose everything. I count it so much garbage, for the sake of gaining Christ and finding myself incorporate in him, with no righteousness of my own, no legal rectitude, but the righteousness which comes from faith in Christ, given by God in response to faith. All I care for is to know Christ, to experience the power of his resurrection and to share his sufferings, in growing conformity with his death, if only I may finally arrive at the resurrection from the dead.
>
> Philippians 3:4–11, NEB

In the power of Christ's resurrection Paul became the greatest missionary the Church has ever known. Whatever the hardships and setbacks, his work was marvellously fruitful, not only in the immediate spreading of the Gospel and the foundation of Christian communities throughout the Mediterranean world, but also in the lasting influence he has exercised on Christian theology, mysticism and practical living. Anyone viewing his achievements from the outside might have summed it up by saying that after notable success as a Pharisaic Jew, Paul had changed his course and made an even greater success of Christian apostleship. So he had, but Paul's own writings tell another story. His desire to share Christ's sufferings was fulfilled in many ways, particularly through his experience of weakness and failure.

Our Second Letter to the Corinthians was apparently written at a time when rival preachers had poached on his preserves at Corinth and made light of his claim to be an apostle.[2] He retaliates passionately, but not by meeting them on their own ground and trying to outdo their lofty pretensions. Instead he almost flaunts his weakness and bodiliness, insisting on these as his credentials; for we have the treasure of the Gospel

> in earthen vessels, to show that the transcendent power belongs to God and not to us. We are afflicted in every way, but not crushed; perplexed, but not driven to despair; persecuted, but not forsaken; struck down, but not destroyed; always carrying in the body the death of Jesus, so that the life of Jesus may also be manifested in our bodies. For while we live we are always being given up to death for Jesus's sake, so that the life of Jesus may be manifested in our mortal flesh.
>
> 2 Corinthians 4:7–11

So far from being a handicap or disqualification, the weakness that belongs to Paul's bodily condition is precisely his hallmark of authenticity as Christ's apostle, because by uniting him with Christ's weakness and death it enables both that death and the power of Christ's resurrection to be continually present. Paul's weaknesses and failures are the place where the power of the risen Christ can shine unhindered; they are therefore necessary to his ministry. Genuinely Christian experience is a catalogue of peril and survival, failure and fruitfulness, as he asserts a little later:

> As servants of God we commend ourselves in every way: through great endurance, in afflictions, hardships, calamities, beatings, imprisonments . . . in honour and dishonour, in ill repute and good repute. We are treated as impostors, and yet are true . . . as dying, and behold, we live; as punished, and yet not killed; as sorrowful, yet always rejoicing; as poor, yet making many rich; as having

nothing, and yet possessing everything.

2 Corinthians 6:4, 5, 8–10

Possibly chapters 10–13 of Second Corinthians were written on a day when Paul was even more upset about his mandate from Christ being impugned. His language is sarcastic and angry as he enumerates his grounds for "boasting": not success or earthly greatness but a list of dangers, privations, narrow escapes, ill-treatment, betrayal, hunger and thirst, cold, anxiety, and weakness suffered with the weak. He admits to something that sounds like a high mystical experience (12:2–4), but immediately adds that he has been afflicted by "a thorn . . . in the flesh, a messenger of Satan, to harass me, to keep me from being too elated" (12:7). Commentators disagree on the precise meaning of this, but evidently he was referring to some pain or weakness or trouble that went with his bodily condition or practical circumstances. Paul regarded it as an obstacle to his work, and

> three times I besought the Lord about this, that it should leave me; but he said to me, "My grace is sufficient for you, for my power is made perfect in weakness." I will all the more gladly boast of my weaknesses, that the power of Christ may rest upon me. For the sake of Christ, then, I am content with weaknesses, insults, hardships, persecutions and calamities; for when I am weak, then I am strong.

2 Corinthians 12:8–10

This is God's view of weakness and failure on the part of people he chooses to do his work. Through these things Christ's Easter victory is proclaimed. They act as a kind of visual aid for the message Paul is preaching, for Christ "died on the cross in weakness, but he lives by the power of God; and we who share his weakness shall by the power of God live with him in your service" (2 Corinthians 13:4, NEB).

This is all very revealing. The experience of Christ's

resurrection and the power of the Spirit are mediated to us, and through us to others, by what seem the most unlikely channels. Pain, misunderstandings, emotional turmoil and confusion, failure and frustration in the good we try to do, tensions with people, the feeling of being unable to pray, the awareness of how our own faults of character sabotage our efforts, disappointment, brokenness and humiliation – all these may be the place where Easter touches us.[3] There can be a ministry of weakness for us, as there was for Paul, because our failures may be needed to manifest the weakness of Christ crucified and the power of his resurrection. The building of Christian community in family, parish, commune or any other group where life is shared takes our prayer and our work; it may also take our weakness, suffering and failure.

The real experience of the paschal mystery in our lives is often like this: not dramatic or obviously heroic, but dull, boring, niggling, and inextricably mixed with people and situations which are partly wrong and things we feel should be different. It is often impossible for us to sort out the mixture of sin and suffering; but we do not need to. The power of the Spirit touches the darkest and most negative experiences of our lives.

In another letter Paul, in a calmer mood, sees this mystery in even larger terms. It is no longer simply an apostolate to a particular Christian community, but a mystical identification with Christ which enables Paul to share the life-giving suffering of Christ, and Christ to continue his redemptive work through Paul:

> Now I rejoice in my sufferings for your sake, and in my flesh I complete what is lacking in Christ's affliction for the sake of his body, that is, the church.
>
> Colossians 1:24

Nothing can be "lacking" in what Christ has done, but he has done it in such a way that we can collaborate with him. Paul "completed" his share in it by martyrdom, his final conformation to Christ. Today many thousands for whom powerlessness is a lifelong condition may be very near to the heart of this mystery.

Paul's experience qualified him to make his greatest contribution to Christian theology, his doctrine of the centrality of Christ and justification by faith. From the moment of his encounter on the road to Damascus, Christ crucified and risen was the centre of his life. He asserted in image after image and argument after argument the identification of every Christian with Christ through faith and baptism, and the consequent union of Christians with one another. We live Christ's life because we have died and been buried with him. Christ lives in us and we in him. Christ and his faithful are one single body, one new man, in whom the one divine life circulates.

Salvation is therefore sheer undeserved gift. We do not earn God's love. We cannot make ourselves right with him by any amount of moral effort divorced from grace; our only access to "justification", or the state of being at rights with God, is faith. As Paul understands it, faith is a willingness to fall into the hands of God with no title to his favour nor any work for which wages could be reckoned due, but boundless trust in his goodness. Faith means the unreserved opening of the human heart to God's promises and God's will; concretely it means accepting God in Jesus Christ. To settle for a do-it-yourself holiness is in the last resort to commit idolatry, because it is to substitute a finite human ideal of perfection for the holy, mysterious, living God, who calls us to a union with himself beyond anything we can deserve or achieve. Our failure may be God's chance to call us away from idolatory to conversion, and thus set us free for himself.

> Let him easter in us, be a dayspring to the dimness of us,
> be a crimson-cresseted east.[4]

6

God's Risk

One of the worst scandals that Christian communities can present to the world is the phenomenon of a person who, after meticulous fidelity to a life of religious observances, has manifestly failed to become human. Among Christian laity and in religious orders one occasionally meets someone who is hardened and sour. Ever since Paul preached at Corinth Christians have been accustomed to the idea that the cross of Christ is a scandal, but de-humanized Christians are a scandal of the wrong kind. It appears that, instead of mellowing them, the very life they lead has made them petty, narrow and rigid. They can be sharp-tongued, hard on other people, unloving and slow to forgive.

This is deeply puzzling. The institutional means established to help people to follow Christ and grow in love seem not only to have failed in these instances but to have blocked natural growth. We wonder what has gone wrong. It is always possible to say that they, and we ourselves, might have turned out a great deal worse without the help of religious institutions. It is certainly necessary to say that God has his secret way into every hardened, shrivelled heart, and that no one knows what may be going on behind an unloving and unlovely exterior. We can think of comparisons like the rough outer shell of a coconut or the prickly covering of a chestnut; we can remember that a beautiful statue is cast within a mould that hides it until the final cracking open. Yet the scandal remains. We must in any case confront the problem, because it may be our own problem too. Pharisaism is an occupational hazard for any Christian.

The Pharisees of New Testament times were certainly not all "Pharisaical"; there may have been many like

Nicodemus. Every human group is mixed, but it is convenient to talk about the risk of religious hardening in connection with the Pharisees, since the gospels so frequently present them in this light. They appear throughout as the focus of opposition to Jesus and as responsible for compassing his death, and this not primarily from political motives, as was the case with the Sadducees, but in the name of Israel's religious tradition. They seem to have known intuitively from an early stage in Jesus's ministry that the revelation of God which he embodied was radically incompatible with the tradition as they interpreted it.

The gravamen of Jesus's accusations against the Pharisees was not that they had over-emphasized the Law but that they had emptied it of its true meaning. A prophet has summed up the whole purpose of the Law in the simple formula: "What does the LORD require of you but to do justice, to love kindness, and to walk humbly with your God?" (Micah 6:8). When Jesus was questioned about the first commandment of the Law, he replied, "You shall love the Lord your God with all your heart, and with all your soul, and with all your mind, and with all your strength"; adding that the second, inseparable from the first, was "You shall love your neighbour as yourself" (Mark 12:30–31). Such a programme is not merely difficult for unaided human nature; it is impossible. This must have been well understood throughout the Old Testament period by countless Israelites who walked humbly with God in prayer and loving obedience, receptive to his grace. Only in subordination to God's free promise and his gift of grace could the Law do its work.

Jesus forcibly pointed out that this subordination had been lost, and with it all sense of proportion in religious matters: "You tithe mint and dill and cummin, and have neglected the weightier matters of the law, justice and mercy and faith; these you ought to have done, without neglecting the others" (Matthew 23:23). The hedge of observances round the Law had become a substitute for its real demands. To carry out with scrupulous attention an elaborate programme of fasts, prayers, Sabbath-keeping and customs concerning dress was humanly possible, and it could be done without "justice and mercy and faith". It could be done without much personal encounter with God.

This is the essence of the contradiction between the Pharisaic distortion of the Law and its real purpose: on the one hand a difficult but theoretically possible programme of self-perfection according to a set of man-made rules; on the other an open-ended relationship with a God who was already revealing himself as holy, loving, tender and desirous of total union with his children. In the one case there was a comfortable ceiling; in the other there was only mystery and a never-ending adventure of worship, love, suffering and joy. In the first case the accent was on moral effort and no explicit reference to God was needed; in the second the believer was drawn into a relationship that was all gift.

God's ultimate gift is the gift of himself in Christ. The life we live in Christ is sheer gift because it is the life of God himself in us, ours simply because of Christ's Easter victory. All the activity of a living thing derives from its fundamental life-principle, and so a human person alive in Christ can at least begin to live up to the humanly impossible standard Christ set: "You must be perfect, as your heavenly Father is perfect" (Matthew 5:48). The "impossible" demands of the Sermon on the Mount, the baffling Beatitudes, are a description of the fruits of God's life in a person open to him in humility and love. Rules there are, for we need discipline under the new dispensation as under the old, but they are guidelines for growth in love, and their observance is meant to express love. What matters is our relationship to the living God.

Since this is our destiny it is clear that to live within institutional Christianity in such a way that one is making observance of the rules into an end in itself is a new Pharisaism, a religion of success that misses the point. Like the older variety of Pharisaism, it is idolatry. It traps us in illusion and closes us against God. This may be the problem with hardened and soured religious people: they can make an idol of their success in apparently keeping the Law, or of the superiority they have established in observing the failure of others to keep it. They may be taking refuge from a risky relationship with a passionately loving God in a safe religious world which they can control and where they feel secure. They can make an idol of perfection. Idolatry is very corrosive for human beings who are made for God. Evangelical conversion is a throwing away of idols to turn to the living God, and it needs to be done again and again. No status, no "way of life", no single decision is enough. But those who are afflicted with Pharisaism are not easily shamed into throwing away their idols, as others might be who make an idol of money or sex. They are failing at least as much as those whose sins are notorious, and they find it much more difficult to recognize their failure.

There are forms of human failure which seem to plunge us directly into the mystery of evil. The soured and hardened products of unloving religious observance are one example, but they seem to take their place alongside many others: the people who have been crushed and embittered by the most destructive forms of suffering we know; the victims of mental suffering which does not seem to ennoble the person or produce any kind of generosity, courage or unselfishness; the children who are abandoned and grow up amid squalor and vice; the wrecked lives which seem never to have had a chance; the young who go to pieces through drug addiction; the suicides. All these incomprehensible tragedies confront us with failure at its most real and most baffling, because there seems to be no core of human meaning left at the heart of the disaster, no person who can be distinguished from the failure. It drives us to the deeper questions: Does God risk failing in human lives? Could it fail, his great enterprise of creation and new creation? Does it fail, will it fail, or succeed for only a minority?

This last is the question that people asked Jesus: "Someone said to him, 'Sir, will there be only a few saved?' He said to them, 'Try your best to enter by the narrow door, because, I tell you, many will try to enter and will not succeed'" (Luke 13:23–24, JB). He does not answer directly; he indicates that it is the wrong question. Yet all down Christian history people have continued to ask it, through controversies on predestination and preoccupation with hell. In the fourteenth century Julian of Norwich, steadfastly believing the doctrine of hell as taught by the Church, was puzzled as to how it could be reconciled with the Lord's promise to her, "All shall be well, and all manner of thing shall be well". She received no clear answer either, but was given a certainty that God's wisdom and love are somehow able to deal with it:

> I had no answer . . . save this: "What is impossible to you is possible to me. I shall honour my word in every respect, and I will make everything turn out for the best." Thus was I taught by God's grace to hold steadfastly to the faith I had already learned, and at the same time to believe quite seriously that everything *would* turn out all right, as our Lord was showing. For the great deed that our Lord is going to do is that by which he shall keep his word in every particular, and make all that is wrong turn out well. How this will be no one less than Christ can know – not until the deed is done.[1]

She holds on to both ends of the chain: the Church's traditional teaching on hell and the assurance of Christ's power to vindicate his promise triumphantly; she cannot see where they meet, and neither can we. To throw away one part of the truth because we cannot see how it fits another part is not advisable; we do better to remain agnostic about their reconciliation and continue to hold both.

In the present instance this means recognizing that ultimate disaster is possible for human beings.[2] To dismiss it with bland optimism or from superficial sentimentalizing of God's love is frivolous and unacceptable, because God himself has taken sin with utter seriousness. The New Testament proclaims the urgency of God's offer in Christ:

Make your way in by the narrow door; these are the last days;
watch and pray; walk while you have the light lest the
darkness overtake you. The cross of Christ gives the lie to any
trivializing of sin and evil. We are bought at a great price;
but we can still refuse to be ransomed. Hell exists as a real
possibility, not because of some arbitrary decision on God's
part but because we have the dark power to create and choose
it for ourselves. Made for God, we can refuse the deepest and
strongest pull of our being, and lock ourselves instead into
hatred and self-centredness. This is hell begun, but on this
side of death our choice is never final and grace continues to
woo us. There is no damnation except self-damnation, but
we can make that our final choice. This is the ultimate – the
only ultimate – failure.

The New Testament has a verb for failing (ὑστερεῖν,
hysterein) which makes this possibility vivid. Its primary
meaning is "come too late", "fail to arrive", "miss", "be
excluded from something because one has not arrived in
time". It is used in three significant places where the risk of
final loss through self-exclusion is envisaged. The Letter to
the Hebrews recalls the example of Israel in the desert: they
sinned and many of them died there, without reaching the
promised land of rest. This should be a warning to Christians
who hold a better promise, says the writer: "Therefore,
while the promise of entering his rest remains, let us fear lest
any of you be judged *to have failed to reach it*" (Hebrews 4:1).
The New English Bible has "one or other among you should
be found *to have missed his chance*". The same thought occurs
later in the Letter, in connection with preserving peace and
charity: "See to it that no one *fail to obtain* the grace of God"
(Hebrews 12:15). In a different perspective, Paul uses the
verb at the end of his indictment of both Jews and gentiles:
"All have sinned and *fall short of* the glory of God" (Romans
3:23).

The same idea, though not the same verb, is present in the
parable of the ten bridesmaids, where the five foolish who
have gone to buy oil arrive too late for the wedding, and
knock on the door in vain, saying, "Lord, Lord, open to us."

The bridegroom replies, "Truly, I say to you, I do not know you" (Matthew 25:11–12). An even more disquieting prediction by Jesus suggests how far self-deception can go in religious practices:

> On that day many will say to me, "Lord, Lord, did we not prophesy in your name, and cast out demons in your name, and do many mighty works in your name?" And then will I declare to them, "I never knew you; depart from me, you evildoers."
>
> Matthew 7:22–23

"*I never knew you*": these professionally religious persons had never allowed the Lord, as Peter allowed him, to know them with the deep, penetrating love that would have stripped them of falsehood and re-created them in grace. So they "arrive too late"; they fail. Even for the thief on the cross beside Jesus it was not too late; he let Jesus know him.

God spends himself in creation and grace, as Jesus spent himself in reaching out to his fellow criminal. God bears us in his womb all through our mortal life, and he risks miscarriage. He hopes and longs for us as he bears us towards our birth into eternal life, more than any woman longs for the birth of her child. Both Old and New Testaments use organic language when they speak of God's compassionate love, or the compassion of Jesus; it is the language of "entrails" or "womb". When Jesus allowed the divine creative love to be incarnate in his human compassion, it was as though the womb of God moved with the labour of the new creation.[3] Could he miscarry?

The truly new thing is always beset with risk. The violinist has never played the sonata as he plays it tonight; the surgeon has never spent all his strength and skill on just this work on this patient before; the lovers have never touched each other before at this depth; the woman has never before borne this child. It is a new project, a new vision, a new creation, a new person. How much more the creative work of God, who alone can bring forth the truly new and unprecedented! He is outside time, to be sure, and there is no past or future in his knowledge; but his creature is free, and the glorious precariousness of creation remains. He takes the fearful risk of giving us freedom.

The Old Testament saw a little of the heart of God as he laboured and loved and risked failure with his beloved. It is told in the story of the vineyard that is Israel. Isaiah spoke a poem about God's lavish care and toil, his high hopes, and his disappointment:

> Let me sing to my friend
> the song of his love for his vineyard.
>
> My friend had a vineyard
> on a fertile hillside.
> He dug the soil, cleared it of stones,
> and planted choice vines in it.
> In the middle he built a tower,
> he dug a press there too.
> He expected it to yield grapes,
> but sour grapes were all that it gave.
>
> Isaiah 5:1–2, JB

Wine was the symbol of joy, and the vine the most carefully tended of crops. God looked for joy in Israel as the fruit of his tender care, but it yielded him sour grapes and no joy. Later in Isaiah there is another poem which seems to open prospects of reconciliation between Lover and beloved:

> That day,
> sing of the delightful vineyard!
> I, Yahweh, am its keeper;
> every moment I water it
> for fear its leaves should fall;
> night and day I watch over it.
>
> I am angry no longer.
> If thorns and briars come

> I will declare war on them,
> I will burn them every one.
>
> Isaiah 27:2–4, JB

God's love for his vineyard has not failed, nor has his hope died, but the matter is unresolved.

Jesus told the story in a different key in his allegory about the wicked vine-dressers. The owner has taken all proper care to provide a wall, a winepress and a watchtower in his vineyard; he then leases it to tenants and goes abroad. Vintage time approaches and he sends a servant to collect his produce, but the man is thrashed by the tenants and sent away empty-handed. The owner goes on trying with servant after servant, but

> they beat some, and killed others. He had now only one left to send, his own dear son. In the end he sent him. "They will respect my son", he said. But the tenants said to one another, "This is the heir; come on, let us kill him, and the property will be ours." So they seized him and killed him, and flung his body out of the vineyard. What will the owner of the vineyard do? He will come and put the tenants to death and give the vineyard to others.
>
> Mark 12:5–9, NEB

This is much grimmer than Isaiah's poems. It is no longer merely a case of sour grapes and no joy, but of no produce at all and a crescendo of malice and violence, ending with the murder of the landlord's son. The telling of the story marks a crisis point in Jesus's life as the Synoptics present it; its meaning is all too plain. The narrative ends with an implication that the covenant privileges of Israel will be transferred to the gentiles, who will yield God the fruit Israel has failed to produce, but there is no real indication yet as to how God's hope and joy will be fulfilled. If the parable or allegory goes back in this form to Jesus himself it is possible that not even he could see how; he may have foreseen his own death but not understood the full meaning and fruitfulness of it. It would have looked more like the darkest of all Israel's failures, the final tragedy in the story of God's love for his vineyard.

The climax of the theme comes at the Last Supper. The three Synoptics record Jesus's word, "I shall not drink again of the fruit of the vine until that day when I drink it new in the kingdom of God": the Jewish Passover meal, and still more the Eucharist which Jesus is about to institute in the setting of the Passover, look forward to the joy of eternity which was symbolized in the Old Testament by a banquet. Then Jesus gives thanks and breaks the bread which he declares to be his body, and blesses the wine which is now his blood and will be poured out for many, that a world's sins may be forgiven. This is the Servant's ultimate self-giving in love; he enacts freely and sacramentally what will be done in starkest reality by the hands of violent vineyard tenants a few hours later.

John does not refer specifically to the institution of the Eucharist at this point, but in the context of the supper discourses he gives the clearest and most profound statement of the mystery of the vine:

> I am the real vine, and my Father is the gardener . . . Dwell in me, as I in you. No branch can bear fruit by itself, but only if it remains united with the vine; no more can you bear fruit, unless you remain united with me. I am the vine, and you the branches. He who dwells in me, as I dwell in him, bears much fruit; for apart from me you can do nothing. He who does not dwell in me is thrown away like a withered branch . . . This is my Father's glory, that you may bear fruit in plenty and so be my disciples.
>
> John 15:1, 4–6, 8, NEB

The beloved Son has been sent to the vineyard, but not on the hopeless errand of trying to collect produce. Israel cannot bear fruit for God except by organic union with Christ, who realizes in himself Israel's vocation to be Son, Servant and beloved Bride of the Lord. In an atmosphere of solemn,

profound joy the secret is told at last. Jesus is not a collector
of dues; he is himself the only real vine, and he will yield the
fruit of love, the wine that gives joy to God and to all God's
household. Only when broken will his body be food for the
world's life; only when crushed will the grape of his life yield
the wine for this joy. "These things I have spoken to you,
that my joy may be in you, and that your joy may be full"
(John 15:11). Our sinful world was closed against God, and
Jesus had to let himself be broken open; he offered himself
joyfully that the life and love of God might circulate freely.

So powerful and transforming was this love, incarnate in
the human heart of Jesus, that in the events of Good Friday
the failure of Israel was the very occasion for God's success.
He was cast out of the vineyard, and crucified outside the
holy city by the authority of the pagan governor. God's last
emissary, his own dear Son, had failed more signally than the
prophets, and Israel had failed to recognize the supreme offer
of God's love and grace. But into Jesus's loving surrender to
the Father not only the people of his own race but every
member of our human family is potentially engrafted. He is
the vine; and branches without number can be grafted in
until the end of time, to bear the fruit of love, that God's joy
may abound and the joy of us all increase without end.

Only in Christ can any of us bear fruit; once away from the
vital sap of the vine we wither, harden and shrivel into
sterility. Here is a key to the problem of why hardening and
embitterment can occur among the Pharisees of any age or
culture. A branch cut off from the main stem, drying up in
isolation from the source of its life, is unlikely to produce
sweet grapes.

It is well to remember none the less that the solemn beauty
and peace of the supper discourses in chapters 13–17 of
John's gospel are probably the result of many years'
meditation on the words and actions of Jesus by the post-
Easter Church. In his breaking open the Spirit was given,
the Spirit who was to lead the disciples into all truth and
bring to their minds all that Jesus had told them.
Enlightened and empowered by the Spirit, and meeting the

risen Christ in word and sacrament, the first generation could look back on the Easter events, and know the present reality of Easter in their own lives, and so begin to understand. Accordingly the story of the vine could be told anew, as it has been in John's gospel, a story no longer of failure, tragedy and bitter disappointment, but of the joyful triumph of love. This is the true perspective, the perspective given to the Church and the evangelist by the Spirit; but to those immediately caught up in the events of the first Easter, and to Jesus himself, things were less clear. We too may fail and lose and suffer, as Jesus did, with no clear vision of how it can make sense or be fruitful. With a longer perspective, the perspective of that eternity to which Easter is the gateway, we shall know.

God asks nothing of us, in our lives or in our prayer, that he has not first accepted himself and taken into his own heart. No risk, no loss, no failure, no emptiness that we can ever suffer comes near to the humble poverty of a God whose servanthood is the expression of his Godhead. His glory is the giving away of self: Father, Son and Spirit exist only in the infinite emptying out of self for one another. In his infinite, eternal being God is utterly unpossessive. Meister Eckhart went so far as to say that the Godhead dwells in absolute poverty that knows no possession, not even the possession of a name, because all our confident naming of God belongs to the economy of his self-revelation. Into this loving poverty of God our failures can now be taken, through the door of Christ's Easter and his Eucharist. The squandered blood of the failed Messiah is the red sign of that joy of God; it is spilt to be the wine of celebration in a wedding feast where love opens out into deeper love, for all of us in God, without end. The branches are pruned by failure now in this time of growth, that the life of the vine may flow through them without hindrance. Our private ambitions and desires may have to die in the process, for the sake of opening us to life.

As long as we remain on this level we can affirm with Julian of Norwich that "all shall be well"; but Julian herself had difficulty in remaining there, and so do we. If the case is stated in purely biblical terms we know there will be a happy ending, precisely because we have been allowed to glimpse it: Christ is risen. We are like certain readers of novels who look at the last few pages first, and then launch into a tale of danger, love, passion, suffering and suspense with the prior knowledge that everything is going to work out and all the good characters will be vindicated and live happily ever after. In real life things are not like this, and the best modern novels appeal to our sense of truth because they end with agnosticism and ambiguity, and avoid tying up the loose ends. Failures and scandals and hard cases really bite because we cannot see how, or whether, they are linked to the mystery of Christ. We live with dark enigmas, unsatisfied and not reassured. Paul anguished over the failure of Israel through three dense chapters of his Letter to the Romans (9–11). He concluded with a hymn of praise to the unfathomable wisdom of God who had used Israel's failure for the benefit of the gentiles and would reconcile Israel in his own time, by a work of love that would be as wonderful as a resurrection from the dead; but we need not suppose that for Paul all was peace thereafter.

We read Christ's story and we know the story of our own lives; faith convinces us that the one has caught up the other so that the two stories are intertwined, and reciprocally illuminating. But we also know that each of us has the dark power to wrench the two stories apart. The ending remains hidden. We cannot tell which of the hardened and shrivelled branches are still in the vine and which are not, or which ones may be grafted in later. We have to be agnostic before the mystery, even to the point of not knowing whether we are in the vine ourselves. If we did know we should be rich, and then perhaps strangers to our self-emptying God who is poor. If we knew the answers we might find ourselves still outside the failure of Christ.

7

A Celebration of Failure

At the heart of our bitterest experience of failure there is an open doorway to the joy of God.

One day when Jesus was celebrating his joy in the friendship of certain marginal people, "the Pharisees and Scribes murmured, saying, 'This man receives sinners and eats with them'" (Luke 15:2). Jesus replied with three stories. The first two are stories of loss, sadness, search, finding, and then a joy that overflows to everyone. An owner of a hundred sheep loses one; such is his concern for it that he is prepared to leave the ninety-nine at risk as he goes in search of the lost one. He finds it, brings it back exulting and calls his friends and neighbours to share his celebration. "Just so, I tell you," says Jesus, "there will be more joy in heaven over one sinner who repents than over ninety-nine righteous persons who need no repentance" (Luke 15:7). Then a woman has a little hoard of ten silver coins, and loses one. She searches with lighted lamp and vigorous broom until she finds it, and then gives a party to her friends and neighbours to celebrate its recovery. Again Jesus ends the story with the refrain, "Just so, I tell you, there is joy before the angels of God over one sinner who repents" (Luke 15:10).

These two brief stories strike the joyful note that rings all through Luke's lovely chapter, but they are only the preludes to a story of far greater loss and recovery, not of a sheep or a coin, but of a beloved son. The parable of the Prodigal Son is a story of failure, disgrace, disappointment and disillusionment; of repentance, return, confession and an explosion of welcoming joy in which all the failure and misery are transformed.

The younger son said to his father, "Father, give me the share of property that falls to me" . . . Not many days later, the younger son gathered all he had and took his journey into a far country, and there he squandered his property in loose living.

Luke 15:12–13

He has had a loving father and a good home, but something has gone wrong, and off he goes. Like many a grief-stricken parent, his father must have wondered, "Where did I fail?" It should not have turned out like this. From the way he speaks later in the story, we know that the father experiences it as bereavement: the son he loved is as though dead. Free from restraints, the boy runs through his money and eventually finds himself on the edge of starvation; for a time he struggles on amid squalor, but the harsh realities of life bring him to a truthful confrontation with himself and his failure:

"How many of my father's hired servants have bread enough and to spare, but I perish here with hunger! I will arise and go to my father, and I will say to him, 'Father, I have sinned against heaven and before you; I am no longer worthy to be called your son; treat me as one of your hired servants.'" And he rose and came to his father.

Luke 15:17–20

He begins his journey home, materially and spiritually bankrupt, and quite unprepared for the love that runs to meet him:

While he was yet at a distance, his father saw him and had compassion, and ran and embraced him and kissed him. And the son said to him, "Father, I have sinned against heaven and before you; I am no longer worthy to be called your son." But the father said to his servants, "Bring quickly the best robe, and put it on him; and put a ring on his hand, and shoes on his feet; and bring the fatted calf and kill it, and let us eat and make merry; for this my son was dead, and is alive again; he was lost, and is found."

Luke 15:20–24

Only when we are as poor as this does God our Father really get his chance. Even in our own closest human relationships the failure of someone we love can be endearing. You want to cherish the person you dearly love, but there is a front of self-sufficiency or competence or impenetrable calm, and you have no opportunity for anything beyond superficial gestures. Then one day the beloved person is in trouble, and at last vulnerable to love. In the weakness, the failure, the need, you can get in and help, not from any superior position or because you think you are any stronger yourself, but because you can be present to the beloved. You can be there, in it, no longer rebuffed, perhaps even needed.[1]

Though God is an almighty lover, he too can find himself shut out, and he too longs to find an open door of vulnerability in us. It is extraordinarily hard for us to realize this, conditioned as we are by a secular ethic of success and a religious ideal of moral perfection which may owe little to the Gospel. God calls us, implants his life in the deepest centre of our being at baptism, and loves us into growth. He does not propose to us some lofty, rigid ideal to which we must attain by our own unaided human resources. We are more sinful than we know, more deeply flawed than we can recognize by any human insight; but grace works in us in the deepest places of body and spirit. We must live from our weakness, from the barren places of our need, because there is the spring of grace and the source of our strength, as Paul discovered: "When I am weak, then I am strong." When we can stand before God in the truth of our need, acknowledging our sinfulness and bankruptcy, then we can celebrate his mercy. Then we are living by grace, and we can allow full scope to his joy.

For many of us it is difficult to live honestly from this place of failure and weakness. Even if we know with our heads that we should, we may still slip back into the old attitudes and behave as though God were expecting us to succeed and making his love conditional upon our achievements. If we have become hardened in such an attitude it may take some deep experience of failure to disabuse us. When a crisis occurs I may find in myself the sheer moral impossibility of obeying God. It is not simply a matter of emotional rebellion, or of knowing that "the spirit is willing but the flesh is weak"; the will itself is unwilling. I am rebellious to the core and do not even want to want God's will. Perhaps I can push it one stage further from me, and say with a kind of tortured effort, "I want to want to want your will", and then ask myself if there is even a grain of honesty or good will in that. I am helpless; and as the father of the epileptic boy cried to Jesus, "I do believe, help my unbelief", so I can only say to God, "I am rebellious down to my roots, help me."

Here, as we teeter on the edge of despair, beset by every kind of temptation and feeling as though we had already fallen, the Spirit is released. This is his own place, the deepest place of our being where he is wedded to our spirit, where he can act and give life, where he can free us from all that hampers the true thrust of our will. God himself creates our freedom; he gives us freedom as his continuing gift of love, and he alone can influence it from within, in no way violating or diminishing it. Entombed Lazarus is a sign not simply of a certain group of people who had obviously closed their hearts against Jesus, but of each one of us. In this hopeless situation, where you are nothing but stark failure, you know the miracle of grace. This tomb is the place of resurrection, and if you believe you will see the glory of God.

The Spirit has to batter through our proud defences, and our hearts are bruised in the process. This is what "contrition" means, the bruised heart set free for its Lover. A poet of Israel knew this, millennia ago, and expressed it in a psalm which tradition ascribed to David in his repentance:

The sacrifice acceptable to God is a broken spirit;
a broken and contrite heart, O God, thou wilt not despise.
Psalm 51:17

Centuries later, John Donne celebrated this painful release in a "Holy Sonnet":

> Batter my heart, three-personed God, for you
> As yet but knock, breathe, shine, and seek to mend;
> That I may rise and stand, o'erthrow me and bend
> Your force to break, blow, burn, and make me new.
> I, like an usurped town to another due,
> Labour to admit you, but O, to no end.
> Reason, your viceroy in me, me should defend,
> But is captived and proves weak or untrue.
> Yet dearly I love you and would be loved fain,
> But am betrothed unto your enemy.
> Divorce me, untie, or break that knot again,
> Take me to you, imprison me, for I,
> Except you enthrall me, never shall be free,
> Nor ever chaste except you ravish me. [2]

We do not know how long it took the Prodigal Son to "come to himself" and decide to go back to his father, or for how many months or years the father watched the road and longed for him. It may take us many years and much wandering to reach this point of breakthrough; it may even take us all our lives. The thief who hung on a cross beside Jesus had taken all his life to arrive at this zero point of failure where he was broken open at last to the love that had waited for him, the love that was ready for him now in his fellow convict. "Jesus, remember me . . ."; it was so brief, and nothing mattered at the end of the day except this. All his failure was transformed; indeed, it had all been necessary, because it had brought him to the emptiness and need of this moment when there was nothing else left for him, when in the depth of his tormented heart the Spirit touched his freedom and he opened himself to grace. His conversion is an extreme and glorious example of what Paul meant by "faith": he has no "works" for which reward could be due, only a grace-empowered openness to grace, a willing receptivity to the gift of salvation.

The only ultimate failure for human beings is the failure to be open to that gift. Only if we "fail to arrive"[3] at that moment shall we be truly frustrated. None of the everyday disappointments we call "frustrations" is worthy of the name, and even the most agonizing of our failures may be necessary if they bring us to the place of breakthrough.

In the joy of Easter the Church plainly says that Adam's sin, in which all our contributions are deemed to be included, was "necessary". It was a "fortunate" or "happy" fault. These statements are made in a highly lyrical passage, but we cannot write them off as poetic licence. Poetry may often serve as a better vehicle for theology than prose; for it may approach nearer, in its own fashion, to the mystery of God, evoking what cannot be captured in any other terms:

> Father, how wonderful your care for us!
> How boundless your merciful love!
> To ransom a slave
> you gave away your Son.
>
> O happy fault, O necessary sin of Adam,
> which gained for us so great a Redeemer![4]

"Happy fault, necessary sin": so the Prodigal Son would have said. If he had not left home, disgraced himself and failed so badly, he might never have known his father as he knew him now. He had never appreciated the dignity that was his or known how precious he was accounted, until he met that lavish love which welcomed him home. He crept back, seeking a slave's status; he was given a son's place and honours were heaped upon him. Such generosity is no wistful dream on our part of how things might be between us and God, no poet's imagination running away with him, but Jesus's official picture of the state of affairs; this is how things stand between us and our Father, because his reckless generosity has found the opening it sought into our lives. It was that "happy fault" which opened the door to his love; and in the light of Easter, joyful and wondering, we can see things for a moment as they truly are. This is the joy Christ promised, the joy no one can take away from us.

In the end our whole experience and all the vicissitudes of our lives will be matter for thanksgiving and joy as we see them through God's eyes, transfigured by his love. Our strength, achievement, growth and success will seem to us beautiful, because they are the Lover's early gifts that have been preparing us for the gift of himself; but we shall rejoice equally in our failures, mistakes, weaknesses and wounds, healed now by the wounds of Christ. Our forgiven sins will be shining tokens of love, like the battle scars which are the pride of a victorious warrior. When Jesus rose from the dead and sought out his frightened friends, he did not come with wounds simply effaced:

> "See my hands and my feet, that it is I myself; handle me and see; for a spirit has not flesh and bones as you see that I have." And when he had said this, he showed them his hands and his feet.
>
> Luke 24:39–40

They were not horrified at what they saw, but full of joy. Those scars were the marks of sin and malice, the imprint of the destruction which human hatred had wrought when it spent itself on Jesus in his passion. The Friday's wounds had been horrifying, but the scars he showed on that Sunday and keeps for ever in his glorified body are transfigured and beautiful. On Easter night the Church prays, "By his holy and glorious wounds may Christ the Lord guard us and keep us." They are proofs of love, tokens of victory, the intercessor's mighty argument on our behalf.

> Scars were upon his feet, his hands, his side.
>   Not, as dulled souls might deem,
>   That he, who had the power
> Of healing all the wounds whereof men died,
>   Could not have healed his own,
> But that those scars had some divinity,

> Carriage of mystery,
> Life's source to bear the stigmata of Death . . .
>
> By these same scars, in prayer for all mankind,
>   Before his Father's face,
> He pleads our wounds within his mortal flesh,
> And all the travail of his mortal days:
>   For ever interceding for His grace,
>   Remembering where forgetfulness were blind,
>   For ever pitiful, for ever kind,
> Instant that Godhead should take thought for man,
>   Remembering the manhood of His Son,
>   His only Son, and the deep wounds he bore . . .[5]

God has dealt, and still deals, with our human disaster not by some omnipotent gesture from afar, but by coming down into it with us and transfiguring it from within so that its whole meaning is changed. During the Second World War a certain Jew in a concentration camp was ordered, amid conditions of the utmost degradation, to clean the latrines. A Nazi guard stood over him, shouting abuse, and then by way of a rough joke pushed him down into the filth. "Well, Jew," asked the guard, "and where's your God now?" "He's down here with me in the dirt", replied the prisoner.

The Prodigal Son, far from home, dirty, lonely and hungry, envying the pigs their swill amid his degradation, is each one of us in our alienated, sinful condition; and he is our whole human race. But he is also the beloved Son of the Father, coming in love and sent by love to identify with us in our extremity of need. Paul uses language of the utmost realism to express this identification:

> God has done what the law . . . could not do: sending his own Son in the likeness of sinful flesh and for sin, he condemned sin in the flesh, in order that the just requirement of the law might be fulfilled in us, who walk not according to the flesh but according to the Spirit .
> For our sake [God] made him to be sin who knew no sin,

so that in him we might become the righteousness of God.
Romans 8:3–4; 2 Corinthians 5:21

These statements are so packed with meaning that they are difficult for us to grasp. Paul is talking about a staggering identification between God's Son and ourselves. He thinks of our human nature (body and spirit alike) as initially closed against God and bereft of his Holy Spirit. This state of alienation from God Paul calls "flesh"; humanity, in so far as it is still "flesh", is dislocated, corrupt, stripped of its dignity and frustrated of its purpose. The lot of "flesh" is pain, weakness, disharmony, every kind of suffering and eventually death. These things, and particularly death, are the signs of sin's work; they belong to the condition of "flesh" as given over to sin, but they are not in themselves sinful. Rather they are morally neutral, ambiguous. This is why God could send his holy, sinless Son "in the likeness of sinful flesh". Christ aligned himself with us and fully shared our lot, refusing no drop of the bitterness of our existence, but personally free from our guilt. He "knew no sin", yet for our sake "God made him to be sin"; made him, that is, a full and unprivileged partaker in the condition to which sin had reduced us, so that he could live it at its rawest, but use these very conditions to express his love. The Beloved Son identified himself with the Prodigal Son, amid the pigs and dirt and hunger, suffering the loneliness and alienation. In the Prodigal's face the Father's likeness, stamped on him at creation, was marred beyond recognition; the face of the Beloved was marred too when as Suffering Servant he "had no form or comeliness that we should look at him, and no beauty that we should desire him" (Isaiah 53:2).

It is Christ who says, "I will arise and go to my Father." Love is not content merely to share our lot; the Beloved Son wants us to share his. There is a journey home which he must make, a passage from this world to the Father, from alienation to union, from "flesh" to spirit, from mortality to eternal life. His identification with us is strong enough to stand the strain; he can draw us with him in his passover. "I will arise and go to my Father . . . Father, I want those whom you have given me to be with me where I am, that they may see the glory you have given me" (cf. John 17:24). His solidarity with us in "sinful flesh" is the means by which in him we can "become the righteousness of God".

The consequences of this "bargain" or "exchange", as the Church occasionally calls it, are so wonderful that most of us are too timid to take them seriously. All my weaknesses and what I am tempted to think my frustrations are engulfed in his. The violence we deplore in our world, and the petty violence we practise on one another or on ourselves, have somehow been absorbed into the violence of his cross; they are no less terrible for that, but they are transformable by the love which there accepted them. In the gasping cries from the cross God spoke his word of irrevocable acceptance, his acceptance of us and our history in a new and unbreakable covenant of love, sealed in the blood of his Son. Wounded humanity is for ever within the Godhead. Never again can God see Adam, who is every one of us, apart from Christ. The identification holds. I fail now, not I, but Christ fails in me.

In the fourteenth century Julian of Norwich had a vision of a lord and a servant:

I saw the lord look at his servant with rare love and tenderness, and quietly send him . . . to fulfil his purpose. Not only does that servant go, but he starts off at once, running with all speed, in his love to do what his master wanted. And without warning he falls headlong into a deep ditch, and injures himself very badly . . . He could get no relief of any sort: he could not even turn his head to look at the lord who loved him, and . . . was so close to him. The sight of him would have been of real comfort . . . His mind was shocked, and he could not see the reason for it all – so that he almost forgot the love that had spurred him on . . . He could not clearly see his loving lord, so gentle and kind towards him, nor could he see how he really stood in the eyes of that same loving master . . . In all this the good Lord showed his own Son and Adam as one man. Our virtue and goodness are due to Jesus Christ, our weakness and blindness to Adam; and both were shown in the one servant . . . Jesus is everyone that will be saved, and everyone that will be saved is Jesus.[6]

In the human face of the risen Christ the image of God shone forth anew, more beautiful than in the Adam who had been God's darling in the beginning.

The rite of sacramental reconciliation ("confession") as practised in the Catholic Church includes a prayer spoken by the priest over the penitent after confession, absolution and the assigning of a "penance":

> May the passion of our Lord Jesus Christ,
> the intercession of the Blessed Virgin Mary, and of all the saints,
> *whatever good you do and suffering you endure*,
> heal your sins,
> help you to grow in holiness,
> and reward you with eternal life.[7]

In other words, your real "penance" is to go on living. Your whole life has been consecrated by the sacrament, because it has been drawn into Christ's Easter mystery. All the good you do: your work, your joy, the love you give and receive, and all you suffer and endure, all your failure, the recalcitrance of things, your disappointments and "frustrations" – all these and everything in your situation are now transfigured, because they are part of the paschal mystery. They will be experienced exactly as before – tedious or joyful or hard or bitter or beautiful or simply ordinary – but they are radically different, because Christ has taken them as his. He must arise and go to his Father, in your life and through your failures. They have become part of the way home. All our wandering with bloody feet since the dawn of human history has led us into his dark journey.

★

When the scarred and radiant Christ stood among his disciples on the evening of Easter Day, he was gathering into a community eleven men who were extremely frightened, confused and shocked. Their fellowship with Jesus during his mortal life had been the first essay in Christian community, and from the beginning it had been a failing community. Nearly every time its members opened their mouths they had revealed their inadequacies; but no failure had been like their last. In the days of Christ's passover the community had disintegrated; when the Shepherd was struck the sheep were scattered. They were too terrified to stand by him, and during the next few days they were dragged through a series of shattering experiences: first shame and fear, then overwhelming grief and shock at his death, then emptiness and desolation, then bewilderment at confused tales from excited women of which they could make no sense. Then Jesus stood in their midst, saying, "Peace". No wonder they were dumbfounded.

He gathered them with no word of reproach, and gave them the peace purchased by suffering. They were forgiven, lifted into his joy, and sent to preach forgiveness of sins to all nations (cf. Luke 24:46–48). John makes it very explicit:

> Jesus came and stood among them and said to them, "Peace be with you." When he had said this, he showed them his hands and his side. Then the disciples were glad when they saw the Lord. Jesus said to them again, "Peace be with you. As the Father has sent me, even so I send you." And when he had said this, he breathed on them, and said to them, "Receive the Holy Spirit. If you forgive the sins of any, they are forgiven . . ."
>
> John 20:19–23

Ever since that day, Christian community has been a place where people fail, and are seen to fail, and are forgiven. It has been a place where the risen Christ stands among us, bearing the wounds of our failures as transfigured scars, and breathing into us the Spirit of the new creation.

We fail before God, and we fail God. We fail before one another, and we fail one another. If what we are living together is really a shared life in Christ, there must be room in it both for the experience of failure and for the recognition that it is in failure that the Easter mystery takes hold. It is not on the further side of all our weakness, in some ideal marriage, some ideal community, where no one fails, that we shall know God. It is here and now, in our actual marriage or family or community, amid all the frailty and inconsistency, that Christ's Easter is experienced as power. In bearing and being borne with, in forgiving and being forgiven, in accepting and affirming others and being accepted and affirmed ourselves, we know the Lord. In men and women as they are, sinful and weak and redeemed, still failing often but allowing Christ's compassion to flow freely among them: this is where Easter happens.

To build a compassionate community you must "suffer together". This is already true of the smallest community: in any loving and lasting marriage there is shared suffering, and the relationship is deepened by it. Or again, some married couples begin in love, and then seem to fall out of love; they stay together, but with in-fighting all through the middle years. Towards the end they sometimes find a strange peace, discovering that they did love one another after all; the "suffering together" has been part of it. A story is told of an elderly couple who reached their Golden Wedding. A reporter from the local paper went round to interview them, but found only the wife at home. He began on her: "Well, Mrs Robinson, fifty years of marriage – that's very remarkable these days . . . Tell me, have you never thought of divorce?" "Divorce?" echoed Mrs Robinson in shocked incredulity. "*Divorce?* Certainly not. Murder, yes, but divorce, *never.*"

If the life of any Christian community is truly compassionate, there are many chances. It is never the end. We may fail many times, but the stable, faithful love of the other or others continues to accept us, and we can slowly allow God to heal us all. The forgiving, optimistic love of

Christ permeates the redeemed cosmos, seeking more and more human hearts to act as new founts of forgiving love and so enable his forgiveness to flow to every broken human being. This is our share in his redeeming work, and we have to learn how to collaborate. A certain ability to forget injuries is a gift from God, and from one point of view it looks like an art in which he himself is expert. A Jewish story tells of a man who frequently committed a certain sin of thought. He was very sorry, and went into the synagogue to tell God so. "That's all right, son," replied God, "I forgive you." The man rose and left, but on his way out of the synagogue he committed the sin again. He rushed back, full of contrition, "O Lord, I've done it again!" And God replied, "Done what?"

This lovely story captures part of the truth, but we need the other side too. There is a sense in which God does not forget our sins, or want us to forget them, because this is not good enough for his love or our need. All that has been said about scars earlier in this chapter implies a special kind of remembering, the remembering of our sins within his healing love and the transfiguration of all our failure. In our small measure we may have to work towards something similar in our relations with one another. Real forgiveness is not an amnesty, not a sweeping under the carpet of things we prefer not to see. It is a deep healing, and like any healing it may take time. Forgiveness is born from a love that embraces other persons as they are, with all the weaknesses and failures that have made up their history and still condition them. Each of us needs this. It is not only for my particular actions that I need forgiving love; I need to be forgiven for being the sort of person I am. Christian community is built on forgiveness and reconciliation, and when the reconciling love of God comes to us through others we become reconciled to ourselves.

"God was in Christ, reconciling the world to himself", and this reconciliation is celebrated in a special way in Lent. One of the most powerful gospel passages used in this season is the beautiful story of Jesus's encounter with the woman taken in adultery. The scribes and Pharisees had set a trap for him, a trap with a human bait. It sprang back on them. Jesus cut through the sophistry and shamed them, though without condoning sin or suggesting that adultery was of no consequence: "Let him who is without sin among you be the first to throw a stone at her" (John 8:7). The scene ends very quietly; as Saint Augustine remarked, great misery and great mercy were left alone together. If this woman had not sinned, she might never have met Jesus.

A significant feature of this episode is that the Pharisees set the scene in such a way that there is a distinction between themselves and the woman. She is the flagrant sinner, and she is made to stand out in the middle, in full view of everyone, while they are the respectable, the righteous. Jesus breaks down this division: "If there is any one among you who has not sinned, let him be the first to cast a stone." He will not tolerate any "We – They" categories in the matter of sinfulness.

This lesson was not forgotten. From about the sixth century a discipline of penance was established by which those guilty of grave sins were granted the status of public penitents at the beginning of Lent. The Church put ashes on them in a symbolic rite of very ancient origin, evoking our mortality and kinship with the earth. Apparently, however, people came to feel that a sharp distinction between the penitents and the rest of the community was unreal. There was no "We – They" about it; all were sinners and all were entering Lent in a spirit of repentance, seeking the grace and renewing power of God. From at least the early Middle Ages all the faithful identified with the penitents, who ceased to be a separate group. The whole Christian community accepted ashes on their heads on Ash Wednesday, and Lent became a celebration of failure in the perspective of Easter. The great realities of Christian life stand out with particular clarity at this time. In the fifth century Pope Saint Leo said in a Lenten sermon:

The paschal celebration is especially characterized by the

rejoicing of the whole Church in the forgiveness of sins.
This forgiveness is given not only to those reborn at this
time in holy baptism, but also to those already numbered
among God's adopted children.[8]

"The rejoicing of the whole Church in the forgiveness of
sins", the rejoicing of the community which fails, but in its
failures meets God – this strikes the unmistakable Easter
note, but it is not only the failing community which rejoices.
The father of the Prodigal Son is God's self-portrait, and his
joy overflows. He runs to meet his son: a slave might run,
scarcely the master of the house; but he is careless of his
dignity. He is recklessly generous. There are no reproaches,
no regrets, nothing but sheer joy.

The son has prepared his confession on the way home:
"Father, I have sinned against heaven and before you; I am
no longer worthy to be called your son; treat me as one of
your hired servants." He is given time for only two-thirds of
it, because his father is hugging him and interrupting, but
what he says is the essential part: "I have sinned against *you.*"
I have failed a person, failed the father who loves me, failed
you. It echoes the great psalm of repentance attributed to
David: "Against you, you alone, have I sinned" (Psalm
50(51):6, Grail). This is the real failure. Mere non-
achievement does not count beside this. To confess our sins
to God is to confront this centrally personal fact in his
presence; and if we do that humbly and honestly it may not
be very important if, like the Prodigal Son, we forget part of
our prepared piece. The sinner who humbles himself before
God is admitting, "Lord, I can't touch the roots of my sins,
or even know them; they are too deep. But you know them
and you can touch them, these deep roots of fear, insecurity,
pride, lack of trust." The Lord can deal with these,
and he runs to meet us with his generous, loving
absolution.

He loves us, but not for our achievements. The boy in the
parable is a disaster. He has squandered the money and
disgraced the family and thoroughly disappointed parental

expectations; but the father brushes all this aside, prepared to squander a great deal more himself, celebrating and welcoming and trying to make it all up to the lad, for sheer joy. God pours out his love in creation. As the shepherd left his ninety-nine and went in search of his lost one, so, perhaps, God disregards his billions of planets and comes in the person of his Beloved Son to find the Prodigal on our earth.

We do not have to "measure up" to what God expects of us. It is rather a matter of "measuring down", down far enough to be empty, hungry and open to the love of so humble and unselfish a God. The boy simply falls into his father's arms. The Father clasps the Beloved who has become one with the Prodigal, the Prodigal who is now for ever the Beloved, and he sings the Easter refrain, "This my son was dead, and is alive again; he was lost and is found."

8

"I Can't Pray"

In spite of the title of this chapter, you can pray. The ability and the need to pray are your most fundamental characteristics; they are given along with your nature as a human person. To be a person is to have a capacity for relationships, and the deepest relationship of all is that which you enjoy with God who creates you, gives you life, and makes you his son or daughter.

At some point in our lives the prayer which has been going on implicitly probably becomes explicit. The relationship which has been real below the surface is now articulated in moments of actual prayer. We begin to consent to a love affair which will stretch into eternity. We are setting out on a journey to God which is also a journey with God; we are beginning a long search for the Lover who has already found us.

We would not be seeking him unless we already in some sense possessed him, and we would not even want to love him unless he had loved us first. Prayer is therefore the response of gifted people. This word "gifted" is used very restrictedly in our culture, as though it were applicable only to the artistic, the athletic, the musical or the possessors of an unusually high I.Q. In truth we are all highly gifted persons, and God's delight is to pour out his abundance on us even more. He is longing to bless and to give, and looking for my empty, open heart so that he can give himself more fully. A psalmist saw this:

> Let them praise his name with dancing . . .
> For the Lord takes delight in his people.

He crowns the poor with salvation.
Let the faithful rejoice in their glory.

Psalm 149:3–5, Grail

We are the poor in whom God takes delight, and we are not even the "deserving poor" of Victorian philanthropy: the hardworking, thrifty and grateful poor upon whom "charity" might properly be exercised. The real poor are often not deserving at all, but feckless, extravagant, wasteful and improvident. An Englishman who was engaged in research on children's games had occasion to stay for some weeks with a very poor family in Portugal. He attempted to pay them for his board and lodging, but had the greatest difficulty in persuading them to take anything at all, although it was clear that they stood in dire need of the money. Eventually he managed it, and returned to England. A few weeks later he heard that they had used the money to buy themselves a grandfather clock. Enraged at this extravagance on the part of a family with numerous children and scarcely sufficient food and clothing, he sent them more money, only to discover later that they had used it to buy a second grandfather clock. The poor do not always behave as their benefactors would wish; but God loves the poor as they are.

God always gives before he asks, and he gives us life before asking us to give our life away. His trinitarian life is infinite giving, and receiving only to give; and it is a life of infinite joy. Christian prayer is a share in this life of the Trinity, however little we may be conscious of it at such depth.

Prayer is the inner space in your life where you stand before God. Even though all your life is lived with him, there must be opportunities for wasting time together, after the manner of lovers. If a married couple spent all their time earnestly working for each other but never found time for simply being together, enjoying each other's company and being available for love, their relationship would probably not grow deeper and the marriage would suffer strain. Prayer is the time when you drop your other activities and give yourself to God directly, when you advert to the deepest reality of your life and celebrate your love with him.

How you go about this does not matter, as long as the encounter is real. Prayer is the most personal of all activities, and it is therefore different for every person. The best advice is the famous sentence, "Pray as you can, and don't try to pray as you can't". We use our intelligence and sensitivity in human encounters, and we need them equally in this encounter of prayer. We can come to God in any shape or mood; we come as we are, not as we would like to be. What matters is that we come in the truth of our being. The masks, disguises and pretences must be shed; we have to let him know us.

This means that there will be in our prayer both joyful recognition of his gifts in us and honest avowal of our misuse of them. Prayer must not be a monologue; we must also listen to God. His word is always loving, but it can speak to us the unpalatable truth. The half-conscious meanness, the self-deception or rationalization, the inconsistency between our belief and our lives: these things are shown up in the light of his presence. We may have thought ourselves too busy to catch his eye during our work, but there is no possibility of evading it now. In this naked, unshielded encounter with God the untruth in us is shown up. Regular prayer brings refinement of conscience and a new awareness of sin.

Our frailty does not disqualify us from prayer. The falls which leave me ashamed and humbled, the weakness which betrays me into betraying God and the general slum my inner life seems to be when I survey it in his presence: all these I can directly bring to him. They are his business, because they are part of my poverty and he delights in the poor. He invites me down from my shaky ladder of pretence, as Jesus invited Zacchaeus down from his sycamore tree, and like Zacchaeus I have everything to gain by accepting the invitation. Down on firm ground I can let him love me as I am.

Willed resistance is another matter, because prayer and love spring from the will. If I am withholding the obedient love I know he wants, I cannot be simultaneously surrendering my will to God in prayer. Mercifully he waits, and his patient love can bring me to the point of wanting (or wanting to want to want) him to help me change my "No" into a "Yes". This too is poverty of spirit.

The "Yes" which we implicitly say to God in the multifarious activities and decisions of daily life is gathered up into the simple act of surrender to his love when we meet him in prayer. Conversely, the "Yes" of surrender in prayer begins to exert a powerful effect on our lives. For most of us in the modern West life is fairly complicated. Each day seems to be composed of hundreds of pieces which we must co-ordinate; all our intelligence and energy are needed to cope with the demands life makes on us. When simple, contemplative prayer becomes a habit we discover that there is somehow a new unity, as though a hidden thread were pulling all these disparate elements into alignment. At the centre of our prayer we want the will of God, and this marriage of our will with his gives new meaning to everything else. There is a quiet pull, like the pull of the magnetic north on the compass needle. We still struggle with, enjoy or suffer hundreds of things, but we want only one.

The obedience learned in prayer becomes a joyful sharing of everything with our Father. Like Jesus, we "learn obedience through suffering", but through every other experience too, as he did. The Father's word comes to us through people and relationships, through work and new discoveries, through the Scriptures, through beauty, friendship, suffering, failure, success and joy. Obedience is not the anxious watching of a slave who fears his master's displeasure, but the free and joyful responsibility of a loved son or daughter. Like Jesus you have to work hard, stretch and be stretched, and use all your mind to find the right way to do things. You have to try something and fail and look for a new approach, trust your Father and constantly let go into his hands.

All the while the secret current of your prayer flows on, giving meaning to everything you do. Still you come to him in many shapes and moods, still you find his love pervading every experience, but you may find that less talking is needed in the time you spend alone with him. So much is understood and taken for granted between you, so much is already built into your love. You can be silent and listen now more than you used to. A little goes a long way now in the matter of words, and often it is more a quiet waiting, a being-present. You come away with little idea of how you spent the time, and to all human reckoning it would seem that you must have wasted it. Yet you are certain that it is the most important thing in your life.

If this were the end of the matter, failure would not hurt much. If all the failures in our lives could be taken back to God in prayer with an immediate, felt assurance that all is well and everything makes sense, life would be easy, but it would not be real. Prayer would have become an escape route from some of the most painful, baffling and ultimately maturing experiences of life. Failure where it hurts is the failure of our prayer itself. As we consent to the developing relationship with God we are invited, like Peter, to "put out into the deep". We find ourselves in dark seas, and although we read charts drawn by other, more expert voyagers, and even derive some glimmers of understanding from them, they never seem quite to fit our own case. There is a constant, humbling impression that though the key to everything lies in prayer, prayer itself is where we are failing. It has become an experience of emptiness and loss. Time and time again our prayer seems to be a non-event.

There are some images that seem, outside the time of prayer, to help a little: we can think of the classical imagery of dark nights and deserts, or of more home-made analogies like the delicious terror of a tiny child thrown into the air above its father's head. The baby chuckles, never doubting that its father's hands will catch it; and we too can trust our Father's hands, though we seem to be falling in space with no support. We can think of the opposite image, that of a child held so close to its father's heart that it cannot see his face. Or again, Scripture sometimes speaks of salvation as abundant rain from heaven, and when you go to prayer you must not take an umbrella, but let yourself get wet through.

An ancient story recorded in Genesis gives an unforgettable picture of a person encountering God:

> Jacob was left alone; and a man wrestled with him until the breaking of the day. When the man saw that he did not prevail against Jacob, he touched the hollow of his thigh; and Jacob's thigh was put out of joint as he wrestled with him. Then he said, "Let me go, for the day is breaking." But Jacob said, "I will not let you go, unless you bless me." And he said to him, "What is your name?" And he said, "Jacob." Then he said, "Your name shall no more be called Jacob, but Israel, for you have striven with God and with man, and have prevailed." Then Jacob asked him, "Tell me, I pray, your name." But he said, "Why is it that you ask my name?" And there he blessed him. So Jacob called the name of the place Peniel, saying, "For I have seen God face to face, and yet my life is preserved." The sun rose upon him as he passed Penuel, limping because of his thigh.

> Genesis 32:24–31

This very mysterious story was probably inherited from pre-Israelite tradition and its original meaning is uncertain. Even as used by the biblical writer it is open to various interpretations, some of which are not to our purpose here. It is, however, a turning point in the life of a man who had hitherto lived by his wits and now found himself locked in dark conflict with a mysterious stranger who seems, at least on subsequent reflection, to be identified with God. Jacob tries to master his adversary by gaining possession of his name, but he fails. His courageous, relentless struggle wins him the blessing of his opponent, but Jacob is lamed and humbled. He is marked for life by this encounter. The ancestor of the chosen people seems to sum up in himself the whole experience of the people Israel which took its name from him, the people who wrestled with God through a long, dark history until the light of Christ dawned and God was seen on earth as a man. We may find that it also speaks to us of our dark encounter with God in prayer.

These parables and images may give us some understanding of prayer, but only at one remove, as it were. They do nothing directly to diminish our bafflement and sense of failure in prayer itself. There we have nothing to hold on to. Saint John of the Cross, the great sixteenth-century mystic, used to repeat, "Nothing, nothing." Nothing that can be grasped with our intellect or senses is God, and he wants to give us nothing less than himself. He tends therefore to withdraw props and assurances; you go to him wrapped and secure in "no-thing", because any *thing* would come between you and the God who loves you, and insulate you against the abundant salvation he wants to give.

Direct assurance that our prayer is genuine is therefore not attainable, and the conviction that "I can't pray" is fairly normal in those whose prayer is contemplative. There are indirect verifications only, especially charity towards others and steady self-abandonment to the will of God. Those who pray faithfully tend to grow gentler and more transparent, and to find a peace deeper than life's troubles, but to seek reassurance about progress in prayer would be to reinforce the ego's desire for security. Such assurances are usually withheld, because the Lover wants to be all to the beloved. There is no fail-proof method of finding God, because as long as we think there is we are clinging to something that is not God. We are still wanting to succeed.

To be told that poverty of spirit, emptiness and unknowing are part of the game is not very comforting, however, because the sting of failure in prayer is that we truly do fail. It feels like our own fault, and so it largely is. If we consent to be caught up by God's love, our sinfulness becomes manifest as it might never have done had we been left to live our little lives undisturbed. Peter and Paul and many another saint discovered this, and so does anyone who goes with God in prayer into the desert of failure. If we covertly supposed that our sense of failure is nothing more than "a trial", or simply an experience of being purified, it would scarcely bite. We should be playing a game, not really finding ourselves exposed to the truth. It is the same with any humbling experience in our lives: we should be cheating if our protestations of sinfulness before God were nothing but an insurance policy, a calculated decision that it is worth saying I am sinful and unworthy, because then God will contradict me and tell me I am not so bad after all. A superficial reading of the reiterated gospel word, "He who exalts himself will be humbled, but he who humbles himself will be exalted" could seem to yield this meaning, but it is unacceptable. God will not contradict me, because he is Truth and I am more deeply sinful than I know. Jesus told a story of a Pharisee and a tax collector to illustrate the reality of prayer. The Pharisee presented God with a list of achievements for which reward might be expected; his trouble was that he had no room for God, nor any perceived need of him. He was making a fair job of do-it-yourself salvation. The taxman had no achievements of the kind he cared to display. He had no claim whatever except his sheer need: "O God, be merciful to me, a sinner." All he could do was make a space for God to be God for him. This was true prayer, and he went home at rights with God; but God did not contradict him or tell him he was being too hard on himself. On the contrary, he had judged truly and he was deeply sinful, but his truthfulness opened him to omnipotent mercy.

We have to fail in prayer because God is God, and no idol. He is not a comforting father-figure fashioned in our own likeness and fitted to our need, one whom we could control and manipulate. We are made for the living God, holy, mysterious, infinite. When he requires humility of us, he is not making some arbitrary demand; he is simply asking us to become like him in his humility and unselfishness, so that we can share his joy unhindered. To live with God and to be like him we have to be emptied of self-seeking even in its most refined forms. We have to go into the desert of abandonment which Jesus entered on the cross. The failures of our lives and our prayer are real, but because of the Easter

Spirit of sonship given to us we can "learn obedience" through them. We have to fail and be lost, because only then do we come near to the utter unpossessiveness and humility of God.

*

Many people who long for God and try to respond to his love in regular prayer believe themselves to be held back from him by some circumstance in their lives over which they have little or no control. It may be a marriage which, though stable and happy, has never yielded the deep satisfaction of spiritual attunement because one partner does not share the other's beliefs. It may be a job or family responsibilities which leave one insufficient time for prayer. Many men and women in religious life suffer from over-busyness as much as those outside it, and carry a permanent sense of guilt as a result. Or again there may be a compromising situation in one's life which is the inescapable consequence of indiscretions in the past. Or it may be poor health. Whatever particular form the problem takes, the person suffering from it is tempted to think, "If only this were different; if only I were free of this hampering factor or that unsatisfactory state of affairs, I could really love God. *Then* I could really pray."

This is an illusion, because God is in this situation with you, in it in every particular detail. Surrender to him in prayer demands a realistic faith that the present moment, with all it contains, is the time and place for doing his will. Clearly you must make all possible efforts to organize your affairs so that you do have time and freedom for prayer. Some islands of silence and stillness are necessary, and obstacles that you can overcome must be sensibly dealt with; but there will always be a hard core of non-ideal elements which cannot be eliminated. These make up your desert.

The desert is some situation in your life which looks negative, where there are no promising signs of growth, where you have no resources, where you are lonely and lost and there are no paths except the ones you make by walking. The desert is something too big for you.

The deserts in our lives do not look spiritually significant, still less romantic. They are not usually self-chosen: one does not decide to go into the desert. One is led there. Israel was led into the desert by the Lord; Hosea in the Lord's name resolved to lead his wife into the wilderness; Jesus was led there by the Spirit. The deserts of our lives seldom appear to be good places for knowing God, and it is difficult to believe that he is present there. A story in the Book of Exodus illustrates this:

> All the congregation of the people of Israel . . . camped at Rephidim; but there was no water for the people to drink. Therefore the people found fault with Moses, and said, "Give us water to drink . . . Why did you bring us up out of Egypt, to kill us and our children and our cattle with thirst?" So Moses cried to the LORD, "What shall I do flith these people? They are almost ready to stone me." And the LORD said to Moses . . . "Take in your hand the rod with which you struck the Nile, and go. Behold, I will stand before you on the rock, and water shall come out of it, that the people may drink." And Moses did so . . . And he called the name of the place Massah and Meribah, because of the faultfinding of the children of Israel, and because they put the LORD to the proof by saying, "Is the LORD among us, or not?"
>
> Exodus 17:1–7

"Is the Lord among us, or not?" Is he for us? Is he God-with-us, Immanuel, even in this dreary situation? Can there be waters of life even in this barren place? This is the challenge of faith. We are called to believe, and to let him be Immanuel. There can be springs of water even here, a gateway to hope even here, in this unlikely place, even if it is your own failures that have created it. The desert is a place where you do not escape from failure; but in it, as Hosea promised, "you shall know the Lord". You may be asked, as Israel was at another moment of crisis and rebellion, to "look steadfastly towards the wilderness" (cf. Exodus

16:10), and there you will see his glory.[1]

The inner wilderness of your own being is the place into which God is leading you in prayer, because he wants to know you and wants you to know him. You must look steadfastly towards it, this desert of failure, of discouragement about prayer, of confusion, weariness, disappointment and shabby sinfulness. Do not run away from it, or evade it by filling the inner void with distractions and noise. Go into your desert with God. Prayer is the time when you confront it directly. You are asked to let him know you in the desert places of your need and failure, because in this way they are opened to his transforming power. Have no shields or insurances against the living God. You have no security except his love for you.

You have to abide in the emptiness, even though your prayer nearly always seems to be a humbling experience of failure. The desert is only the desert when it is too big for you. God comes with us into our wilderness and feeds us there, but his grace is like manna: unpredictable, precarious, yet always sufficient to our need. If you abide there you will know his mysterious presence, and the wilderness will become a place of springing water. By your fidelity to prayer, the desert can be transformed; and not your own desert only, but the deserts of today's world.

Modern society has the desert always with it. For part of the time we can pretend it is not there, and put our faith in the competence of technology to cope with all problems; but there are some which prove intractable. In certain crises technology fails to deliver, not because of any inadequacy of its own but because we lack the wisdom to direct and use it rightly. We are conspicuously failing to solve the problems of world hunger and to build true peace, because these are ultimately not material but spiritual problems, and we lack the spiritual resources to deal with them. We need a new heart. Lack of resources and loss of direction are precisely the characteristics of desert wandering. Behind these vast problems are the private deserts of so many personal lives: the apathy of the hopelessly poor, the despair of those who find no meaning in their lives, and the anguish of those who once found meaning but seem to have lost it amid failure and disaster.

Between these deserts of modern life and the desert of contemplative prayer there is a vital connection. God's secret grace pervades human history and is at work in our modern world in manifold hidden ways, but it seeks here and there a focus, a place where someone will explicitly consent to what is general and implicit. The hopeless drug addict may awaken after death to find that his head was on Christ's shoulder throughout his failing life, but God seems also to want believers who will freely allow themselves to be led into the desert of failure and there know God. The world needs people who are willingly open to the Spirit in their experience of failure and are brought by it to the point where they can say, "Abba, God of my failure, in this you know me and I know you at last."

There is a parallel between the vocation of a prophet in Israel and that of a contemplative today. In chapter 3 of this book it was suggested that a prophet was both sent to Israel with God's message and identified with Israel in the truth of its life before God. This is especially clear in the cases of Jeremiah and the Suffering Servant. Similarly Christ's apostles were sent to preach the resurrection and the forgiveness of sins, but also called to embody the mystery of Christ's weakness and cross in their own lives; so Peter and Paul signally failed in some respects, and thus became living signs of the power of Christ's resurrection. This pattern of ministry continues in the Church. The life and hope that flow from Christ's Easter must be mediated in every possible way; and all the effort to evangelize, heal, solace, feed and relieve the penury of humankind are "sacramental" signs of the power of life that has broken loose among us since Easter. The new life can work through science, technology, social services, just administration, the arts, education and every adventure of the human spirit which makes life more human for God's children. Nevertheless, the power of Easter must also find its scope in our weakness and failure; and today's society, so oriented to success and prosperity, is not good at finding symbols for this. There is too much cover-up: in both individual and public life people tend to hide failure and to be embarrassed in the presence of death. We need prophets who can confront failure, prophets who, identified with our bankrupt emptiness and experiencing it in themselves, can yet take this very experience into their deepest hearts and find there the heart of God. We need men and women of prayer who can find in defeat and failure the place for knowing God and being open to him, and so can themselves become open gateways between God and our world. We need people who will answer our question, "Is the Lord among us, or not?" as Moses answered it, and open springs of water in our deserts. Such people lovingly assent to the truth which our society conspires to cover up; they face it with us, deeply committed to suffering and failing humankind.

No compassionate "aid" can be effective without some real immersion of this kind in the human predicament. Truly creative response comes from people who have allowed themselves to be drawn deeply into the human condition and have there struggled for meaning, rather than from those who proffer ready solutions from above. Contemplation and compassion are near kin.

In this perspective we may come closer to understanding intercessory prayer. No Christian can dodge this issue, for the New Testament proclaims on nearly every page God's pleasure that we should pray to him for one another and for all our needs. Yet failure in prayer becomes here more tangible than ever. Our prayers often do not seem to be answered. There are people and situations that we have been praying about for years; they have not apparently improved. There are hard cases for which we feel impelled to pray, without any visible result at all. There is the seemingly pointless suffering which we feel powerless to alleviate, and the encounters which we terribly mishandle even though we have prayed.

These baffling experiences are one avenue into a mystery far too large for our understanding, the mystery of God's redeeming love at work in the world and of the "filling up in our flesh of what is wanting to the sufferings of Christ". Since we have not nearly enough data to know what effect our prayer is having, or what part it plays in the whole loving scheme of things, it is sensible to pray as God wants us to, and be content not to know at present. Our faithful perseverance may be the instrument he has chosen to use for the work of his grace. Further, there are occasions when we can be glad, ten or twenty years on, that God did not give us precisely what we prayed for, because in the meantime that issue has been bypassed and we have been led into something much larger; if this is sometimes the case we should be willing to think that it is true in other instances as well, where we do not yet see it. When Martha and Mary sent their messages to Jesus about Lazarus's illness, they were implicitly asking, "Please come and heal him". Their prayer was not heeded; Jesus did not even hurry to Bethany, and his attitude must have seemed incomprehensibly heartless. The bystanders asked, "Could not he who opened the eyes of the blind man have kept this man from dying?" (John 11:37). Yes, he could, but he did not, because he intended to give something greater.

Jesus illustrated the efficacy of persevering prayer by his stories of the widow who pestered the judge until he gave her what she wanted, and the man who went to beg from his friend in the middle of the night. Persevering faithfulness is needed, then; but we have to learn how to pray faithfully without fuss or anxiety, for Jesus also told us not to heap up many words, and not to be worried. Our word "worry" is derived from the Old English *wyrgan*, meaning "to strangle"; it suggests a dog seizing a sheep by the throat and shaking it, a vivid image of what we can do to ourselves. Persevering prayer is not "worrying" but a peaceful abiding in trust as we hold our loved ones in God's presence. On the surface we may still feel desolate and devoid of understanding, but in our deepest heart we will to trust God.

Deeper than any distress in our prayer is the certainty that we are loved. Deserts, darkness, quest: these images tell only part of the story. As the Israelites were very close to the promised land throughout their desert wandering, so we already have what we long for, and as we stumble on we are already at home, because we are in God and he is in us. Our union with him is so intimate that Jesus used the image of a vine: between the vine and its branches there is mutual belonging, a single shared sap, organic union. One single life courses through trunk, branches and tendrils; the grapes that yield the wine of joy are the fruit of this one life. The branches need not worry, for all they have to do is to abide in the vine, and fruitfulness follows. As Jesus tries to tell his disciples the most important things of all, the things they must remember even if they forget nearly everything else he has told them, there is magic in the word "abide":

> I am the vine, you are the branches. He who abides in me, and I in him, he it is that bears much fruit, for apart from me you can do nothing . . . If you abide in me, and my words abide in you, ask whatever you will, and it shall be done for you. By this is my Father glorified, that you bear much fruit, and so prove to be my disciples. As the Father has loved me, so have I loved you; abide in my love. If you keep my commandments, you will abide in my love, just as I have kept my Father's commandments and abide in his love. These things have I spoken to you, that my joy may be in you, and that your joy may be full.
>
> John 15:5, 7–11

The condition for fruitfulness is abiding in him, and abiding is made possible by obedience. Christ's Easter life is perfect joy because every fibre of his body and his human mind is flooded with the self-giving love that is the glory of God's life within the Trinity. This is what his obedience is, and Easter reveals it. Our surrender to God's will in prayer is costly, but it is part of Christ's obedience, and already it is caught up into his joy.

The allegory of the vine was always a story of failure until Jesus applied it to himself. It became a song of joy because his obedient love transformed human failure. If we abide in him and he in us, all our failures are enfolded in his peace, not least the failure of our prayer.

Stillness and peace seem to be characteristic of this abiding, yet in these same discourses at the supper there are dynamic images as well. Jesus speaks of going to the Father; he tells the disciples that he is going away and will return to them, and that he will come again and take them to himself. In Christian prayer we know both sides of this Easter reality. Our prayer is a passover as in Jesus we return to the Father; hence it demands of us conversion, repentance and fidelity throughout a long, dark journey. At the same time it is an eternal abiding in God even now; for Father, Son and Spirit have made their abode in us. Jesus is both "the Way" and "the Vine". If our prayer is fully Christian, both elements will be present. The Easter stories capture both the movement and the stillness.

One of the greatest of the "movement" stories is Luke's account of the journey to Emmaus on the Sunday evening. The stranger who joined the two travellers did not seem to understand why they were worried, and they asked him whether he had not heard about the crucifixion of Jesus. The Israelites' question in the desert, "Is the Lord among us, or not?" pales beside the irony of asking the risen Jesus on Easter Sunday whether he has heard about the crucifixion. Yet it is really the same question, transposed. In neither case could suffering people quite believe that their journey, their disappointment and their bewilderment were shared by the God who was their fellow wayfarer. You and I are apt to ask a similar question in our bad moments.

The two travellers had failed to believe in the resurrection, failed to find out more for themselves, failed to recognize Jesus and failed to understand the Scriptures, yet throughout their long walk the risen Christ was with them, sharing his Easter understanding with them, trying to open their bemused, frightened minds to the glory of his Easter, and theirs. "Don't you see . . .? Don't you remember that the Scriptures pointed to this? It is no accident; this is what they were trying to show: that God's Son, God's Christ, must suffer, and only through that gateway enter his glory. Let go of your plans, your hopes, your restricted, puny ideas. Your Father's love for you is greater than your hearts can conceive, because it is inseparable now from his love for *me*."

The identification holds. Christ's passover to the Father is our passover; Christ's long, dark journey is ours, and ours is his. He is in us and we are in him. In no part of the journey and in no place of failure are we ever alone. It is joyful because of him; there is great beauty along our road, and the certainty of his love. Prayer is our willing communion with a mystery of love far greater than our ideas or hopes or plans or vision, and as we fail bitterly in life and in prayer itself we are gently helped to bypass our limited expectations. Distress and bewilderment, knowing yet not knowing, the burning hearts, the realization afterwards that amid all the unknowing we did know, the closeness of Christ in word and sacrament: all this is an inspired picture of how things are, since Easter, along our road. He is more than a wayfarer with us; he is the Way.

Prayer is a long search, a dark journey; if we think of it as a journey to God we are not altogether wrong, but it is also a journey with God and a journey in God. He is not someone over against us, with whom we have to conduct a conversation or form a relationship. "In that day", said Jesus, the day which dawned at Easter and will see us into eternal life, "in that day you will know that I am in my Father, and you in me, and I in you" (John 14:20). There is nothing, "no-thing", between you and God.

9

The Eastering Spirit

A married couple were taken on as joint gardeners by the owner of a very large estate. It had vast possibilities but was as yet undeveloped. The owner knew they were gifted enough to make something beautiful out of it, and he put the whole complex responsibility in their hands. They were to have great freedom, but he wanted them to keep in touch with him. He meant them to enjoy it, to make a success of it, and to become his trusted friends as the work proceeded.

The estate was the planet Earth, and their names, as will be evident already, were Adam and Eve. They and their descendants were meant to find God, and to be found by him, in success. God made them in his image, provident, intelligent and creative. They were spiritual beings, but thoroughly at home in their finely tuned bodies, and therefore able to use their bodies for creative work, communication, learning, the expression of beauty and love, and the exploration of their world. They were called to grow and to discover, to try and to achieve. They had immensely complicated brains and good eyesight. Their hands were very versatile, unspecialized in structure but capable of extraordinary sensitivity and skill in the service of their minds. The human hand is the primary tool, and with it they built civilization. Into human hands our whole destiny has been entrusted.

They learned to build shelters, and ultimately cathedrals. They discovered how to plant seeds and grow crops. They learned to communicate across time and space by the manual skill of writing, and later they invented computers. They struggled to understand, ever questioning and searching for wisdom. With their minds and hands they healed, caressed and comforted; they built boats and explored their planet. Envying the birds, they made themselves wings more powerful than an eagle's; they walked on the moon. They painted and played music; they wove cloth and carved wood and stone; they threw clay pots and experimented with shape and form. Fascinated by this last experience they conceived of God as a master potter, who had fashioned them out of clay:

> The LORD God formed man of dust from the ground, and breathed into his nostrils the breath of life; and man became a living being.
>
> Genesis 2:7

This was much more than primitive fantasy. They knew that the human equation was dust plus breath-Spirit of God, they knew that they could make things beautifully and responsibly, that they could dream dreams and see visions and give form to them. They knew they were like God.

Through many experiences and the great surge of human energy they were discovering how glorious was the marriage of spirit and matter in themselves, and how they could mirror its glory in the things they made. Some of them grew very beautiful, as their maturing spirits shone out in love through their eyes and faces and every movement.

Collaboration between them became more and more elaborate and sophisticated. They discovered that many enterprises were possible through shared effort and the pooling of resources; they also realized very early that each individual needed the caring love of the others in order to grow. In harmonious co-operation of all kinds they were more than the sum of their individual efforts, and new riches of humanity were disclosed to them. In all this great adventure they were drawn on by the will to succeed, to know, to live. God blessed them, and enjoyed their joy. It was all part of his creative love, and he saw that it was very good. His co-workers knew that they were trusted. Their God was not a "God of the gaps", to be invoked only in the failure of their enterprises or in their times of weakness. He loved their strength, their inventiveness, their leaping intelligence, their growth to maturity.

Unhappily the married couple to whom he had entrusted the estate decided to set up business independently. Their numerous descendants were in full agreement with this policy; and a rival establishment, promising certain immediate profits, was set up. Its records fill much of the Old Testament and the history of all nations for many centuries afterwards. The gifts which men and women had joyfully used in friendship with God now twisted in their hands. Wine had been for celebrating joy, but now it led Noah into drunkenness and degradation. Building and co-operative enterprise had thrilled them, but the project of the Tower of Babel did not turn out well. The grain, wine and oil of Canaan were not recognized as gifts from God and signs of his blessing on human work; they were sought instead within the closed system of the Baalim and so became a seduction to idolatry. The gift of sex, in which joy, responsibility and creativity were powerfully focused, was snatched and debased; once divorced from the meaning and destiny of the whole human person it too became an idol. Even the God-given Law of Israel could be perverted into an idol when it claimed a spurious autonomy. The wrecks of institutional failures littered the landscape for centuries before the fuller reason for their existence began to be apparent: so the Israelite monarchy failed and the temple failed. Even the Lord's vineyard, Israel, did not produce the expected sweetness.

Among the gentiles it was the same story. What the Law was to Israel, philosophy was to the Greeks. The wisdom of God had been scattered among them like seed; his Word was the true light enlightening every human being. The rationality and truth of things could speak to everyone who walked with God in integrity of heart; but gentile wisdom itself went astray into sophistry and pride, misleading those who searched. There was still so much beauty, and they fell in love with it, forgetting its Creator. They quarrelled and fought. All the while their cleverness was growing, until they began to find they had more power in their hands than they could control. It was not weapons that made wars, but human beings, because they needed wisdom to guide the activity of their clever hands and brains, and once they turned their backs on it their artefacts became dangerous. They reached a point where they held the power to destroy the whole estate and all the life it bore, and they were afraid.

Meanwhile they misused their cleverness in other directions. They wrought ugliness where there had been beauty spots, and they made slums. Some of them grabbed far more than their share of the fruits of the estate, so that the majority were hungry and many starved to death. Some of the young among them, being miserable and bewildered, smashed things mindlessly, because it gave them an illusion of power. Others polluted the air, the water and the soil, and used up the forests and fuel of the estate greedily. A few tried to coerce others by torture, of the body or the mind. They were making chaos, and it mirrored the chaos they were.[1]

The Word of God, in whom and through whom all things were made, he who had been revelation to the Jews and wisdom to the gentiles, he whom all humankind had confusedly sought from beginning, now became flesh and immersed himself in the human predicament. He made himself unguardedly vulnerable to the worst that human hands and brains could do, to the full impact of their hatred, frustration and destructiveness. But in his hands was the work of the new creation.

Jesus was a craftsman for most of his life, and he probably had the kind of hands a skilled craftsman usually has: strong, sensitive and very gentle. He used them in significant ways during his ministry, touching untouchable lepers, putting his fingers into deaf ears, moistening a dumb tongue with spittle, and daubing wet clay on a blind man's eyes in a gesture reminiscent of the potter-God who had created them. He linked his healing work with the Father's continuous creation: "My Father is working still, and I am working" (John 5:17); but they were like stolen victories, these

healings, these many times when he used his creative hands
to give health, forgiveness and freedom. The great work was
still to be done. At his last meal with his disciples he rose
from table "knowing that the Father had given all things into
his hands", and with those craftsman's hands washed the feet
of the Twelve. He was doing a slave's job and it embarrassed
them, but it was an acted parable, a symbol of his identity
as the Servant of the Lord who would suffer and give his life
for the many.

Then he went out to his work. Soon the hands of his
enemies were on him, in the darkness of the garden where
they effected a confused and clumsy arrest, through the long-
drawn barbarity of the trial and the manhandling behind the
scenes. Savage hands struck, stripped and scourged. Pilate
washed his hands in public to show that it was none of his
business. Eventually Jesus's hands were nailed, perhaps
through the wrists obliquely rather than the palms. The
Lover's arms were outstretched in a would-be embrace for
all the world: "All day long did I spread out my hands unto
a disobedient and gainsaying people" (Romans 10:21, AV).
This is the visible, external aspect of the Friday's work. The
inner truth is revealed by one of his last utterances: "Father,
into *your hands* I commit my spirit." The un-making
wrought by the cruel, destructive hands of men can be used
for the work of love, the work of re-making a broken world,
because Jesus has made it the means of his surrender into the
hands of his Father.

When he came back to his friends he had been down to the
deepest, darkest, most hopeless and lifeless places,
harrowing hell and bringing the countless generations of the
dead into his presence, yet he could sit and talk and eat with
his own; he could build a fire and prepare their breakfast. He
used his scars to convince their staggering minds, inviting
Thomas's hand with his own: "Know the place of the nails,
and believe."

Over the apostles' personal chaos and the chaos of the
whole sinful world Christ breathed the Spirit of the new
creation: "Receive the Holy Spirit. If you forgive the sins of

any, they are forgiven" (John 20:22). There is an immense work still to be done, for the resurrection is a process spreading onwards and outwards, through every generation and every century, to the spirits and bodies of human beings and at last to the whole material cosmos which is intimately bound up with our life and destiny. All of these are to be "en-Spirited" by the risen Christ, and he calls the apostles to collaborate: "As the Father has sent me, even so I send you" (John 20:21).

The work is a building project more glorious than human ambition ever envisaged, the building of the new Jerusalem which will last for ever. This will be God's supremely beautiful achievement, and ours too as we bear our part. Every person's contribution is needed; no act of love in all human history will perish or be wasted. The new Jerusalem will be "the dwelling of God with men"; yet this image is not enough, for the city will also be the commonwealth of those transformed by love, God's family, the marriage of the Lamb with the whole Church, the wedding feast of eternity. The city will be a living person, the one Christ with all his members grown to perfect maturity. It will be the Body of Christ built and indwelt by the Spirit.

As the Spirit overshadowed Mary to build from her flesh the human body of Jesus, so he is now breathed into all of us, his Easter people, to build us into Christ's mystical Body. He forms in us the mind of Christ so that we come to love the will of the Father as Christ loves it. The joyful obedience of the risen Christ is a vast, pervasive energy of love, intensely personal and creative, which irradiates a wounded world. It calls for our participation. "Creative", like "gifted", is a word used today with too restricted a reference: we can all be obediently creative if we will. The building of Christ's Body is our real work, our great responsibility and our high dignity. We are made for greatness and God knows us at our best. We need to look hard at what real failure is (as opposed to imputed failure), and then be very daring in our lives, unafraid of failing in any other way.

As we share the work, we are being new-made ourselves.

We are God's unfinished work of art:

> Lord of living and dead;
> Thou hast bound bones and veins in me, fastened me flesh,
> And after it almost unmade, what with dread,
> Thy doing: and dost thou touch me afresh?
> Over again I feel thy finger and find thee.[2]

Every time we labour at any human task, struggling, trying to understand, using all our strength and courage and walking humbly with God, and we succeed in our undertaking, we have contributed to the work of the new creation. Every time we watch the death of something we have perseveringly toiled to build, dying a little ourselves but dumbly consenting, we contribute to the great work. Every time I do my best and fail, but allow Christ to take my failure into his, I am contributing. Every time we look back over some enterprise into which we have put our hearts and our years, and see that we have succeeded a little and failed a little more, that success and failure are inextricably intermingled, and that all of it is encompassed by a love greater than we ever suspected, we are being allowed a glimpse of the risen Christ at work through his Spirit.

> How far high failure overleaps
> the bounds of low success.[3]

Like the risen Christ, we are scarred. Our scars seem to hamper us and we fail, but within his obedience our failures are transformed. They are even necessary. The eastering Spirit is within them and over them, and in God's sight they are glorious, though not in ours. Here is another parable. I walked in a field in the first really cold days of October. There had been night frost, a raw and bleak morning, and damp fog. By the middle of the day the sun had come through brightly but was giving little warmth. Everything spoke of the dying year: the falling leaves, the cold, the anxious birds. It was afternoon now and the sun was in the south-west as

I walked along a path on the east side of the field; between me and the sun was a great expanse of cold, wet grass. Suddenly I had the angle right, and for the first time I saw the whole field spread with silver cobweb: a gossamer, light-as-air veil of glory over every tuft of grass, the whole field dancing, dancing.

God's glory clothes creation, and the eastering Spirit is already transfiguring our mortality, though our angle of vision seldom allows us to see it. Under sacramental signs the same mystery of death and life and hidden glory is proclaimed. The gifts we bring to the Eucharist are the fruits of our success: the bread which earth has given and human hands have made, the wine which is the fruit of the vine and the work of human hands. They are signs of growth and fecundity, the products of our successful agriculture and technology. Yet they are signs also of the ambiguity of our life in this time until Christ comes again, for even as we bring our bread and wine they are shadowed by our terrible failure to distribute the earth's food and resources justly. Pain is part of Eucharistic experience. Both our success and our failure are taken into the hands of Christ, and upon them the Spirit is invoked. These gifts which stand for ourselves in all our ambiguity, these failing selves, become Christ's Body.

Only beyond death will the tensions be resolved between our success and failure, our growth and diminishment, our life and the constant little deaths which shadow it. But it is life from beyond death which the Eucharist gives us even now, Christ's life which has been through death and proved itself the stronger, a life enriched by death. So Christ links the gift of the Eucharist with a promise of our own resurrection: "He who eats my flesh and drinks my blood has eternal life, and I will raise him up at the last day" (John 6:54).

In spite of the fearful precariousness of creation, God believes in the power of life which he has planted in us amid so much risk. The grain of wheat risks absolute loss and seems indeed to die in the dark, cold earth, but it is charged with the energy of hidden new life, and its time of glory will come. So the kingdom of God is being built, secretly and with the everlasting patience of love:

> Jesus said, "The kingdom of God is as if a man should scatter seed upon the ground, and should sleep and rise night and day, and the seed should sprout and grow, he knows not how. The earth produces of itself, first the blade, then the ear, then the full grain in the ear. But when the grain is ripe, at once he puts in the sickle, because the harvest has come."

Mark 4:26–29

The spring winds awaken the earth and the rain softens it, making it receptive to the life-laden seed. Both wind and water are images of the Spirit, powerfully breathed and abundantly outpoured to make us receptive to God's seed-word. As a gardener uses broken down organic material to enrich the humus, so the Spirit uses our failure and weakness and our forgiven sin to build in us a receptive humility. Nothing is wasted. In the earth of our flesh and our minds, and so in the earth of our planet, God has sown his powerful Word:

> As the rain and the snow come down from heaven
> and do not return there until they have watered the earth,
>   making it blossom and bear fruit,
> and give seed for sowing and bread to eat,
> so shall the word which comes from my mouth prevail;
>   it shall not return to me fruitless
> without accomplishing my purpose
>   or succeeding in the task I gave it.

Isaiah 55:10–11, NEB

How nearly it might have been "fruitless", smothered by the cold, inert soil; but no, it will *succeed*. Within our very failures God's plan of love is going forward, and will not fail.

The dying of everything around us and within us saddens us still, although we hold this promise of eternal life. Our hearts protest at the fragility of all that is lovely: the spring passes, the daffodils turn brown, the dawn chorus fades away, a tiny unfledged bird falls out of its nest, and a beloved person grows old and dies. We strive for life and survival and success, but we know that the experience of them on this side of death is too elusive. Our successes in this present time are pledges and firstfruits, like the healings Jesus wrought before his passion. They point us towards God's success, towards the completion of the work he is patiently pursuing. To Julian of Norwich he said:

> See, I am God; see, I am in all things . . . See, I lift never mine hands off my work, nor ever shall, without end.[4]

The final success will be an achievement which has been through utter failure, through the narrow gateway to hope, and come out victorious. God will wipe away all tears, and there shall be no more death, no more failure.

* * *
* *
*

Notes

Notes

1. Only One Chance?
1. St Thomas Aquinas, wise man that he was, prescribed as remedies for sadness the sympathy of friends, the contemplation of truth, sleep and baths (cf. *Summa Theologiae* Ia, IIae, 38, 3–5).

2. God's Friends Sometimes Succeed
1. Some resemblance might be detected to the ideal product of English public schools of the nineteenth and twentieth centuries.

3. Prophetic Failure
1. While it is generally agreed that Hosea was the first prophet to use nuptial imagery for the covenant relationship between Yahweh and Israel, it is less certain that the first three chapters of his book are to be understood in the traditional way assumed here. Some scholars believe that the woman who is Hosea's wife and the mother of his children is a different person from the slave or prostitute he buys and disciplines; and that it is the redactional work of a disciple which has made the whole story seem to be about Hosea's marriage. If this view were correct, Hosea's message would be the same, but it would be less directly derived from his personal suffering.

2. Walter Brueggemann, *The Prophetic Imagination* (Philadelphia, Fortress Press, 1981), p. 58. This book gives precious insights into Jeremiah's "ministry of articulated grief" (*ibid.*, p. 53).

3. Isaiah 42:1–9; 49:1–6; 50:4–11; 52:13–53:12. These occur within that part of the book (i.e. chapters 40–55) attributed to an anonymous prophet we call "Second Isaiah", dating from

about the middle of the sixth century BC. Whether the Servant Songs are also by Second Isaiah is debated; probably they are, but they may have been inserted some time after the composition of the main text. Much critical work has been done on this and other questions concerning the Servant Songs, which can only be presumed here.

4. There is a parallel. Asking this crucial question, John faced death in squalid circumstances, apparently forsaken by Jesus, to whose cause he had dedicated his life. Jesus, asking the agonized question, "My God, my God, why . . .?", also died in squalid circumstances, apparently forsaken by the Father, whose love had been the lodestone of his life.

4. *The Failed Messiah*

1. Ralph Wright, "Two Trees", in *Life is Simpler Towards Evening* (Francestown, New Hampshire, The Golden Quill Press, 1983), p. 65.

2. From "Lord, it belongs not to my Care", by Richard Baxter (1615–1691). Quoted from *The Oxford Book of Christian Verse*, ed. by Lord David Cecil (Oxford, Clarendon Press, 1940), p. 217, capitalization altered.

5. *Let Him Easter*

1. This episode of a great catch of fish is very like one recorded in the last chapter of John's gospel, after the resurrection. Possibly Luke has anticipated it; possibly something of the kind happened twice. We cannot be certain, but there is symbolic fitness in this framing of Peter's companionship with Jesus by two such scenes at the lake.

2. Some scholars think 2 Corinthians a combination of two or more Pauline letters.

3. Compare Hilaire Belloc's remark: "I do not believe that good men have quiet consciences. I hold that an uneasy conscience – at any rate nowadays – is the first requisite for Heaven, and that an inflamed, red, feverish, angry conscience is a true mark of

increasing virtue. I have met many men with quiet consciences, not all of them wholly unintelligent, but nearly all of them scoundrels" ("On Rasselas", in *Short Talks with the Dead*).

4. G. M. Hopkins, "The Wreck of the Deutschland", quoted from *The Faber Book of Religious Verse*, ed. Helen Gardner (London, Faber & Faber Ltd, 1972).

6. *God's Risk*

1. Julian of Norwich, *Revelations of Divine Love*, translated into modern English with an Introduction by Clifton Wolters (Harmondsworth, Penguin Books, 1966), chapter 32.

2. Which is not the same thing as believing that any particular person has been or will be damned, even Judas.

3. There is paradox in this imagery. According to one traditional line of thought, death is our birth into eternal life, and therefore our mortal existence could be called our ante-natal period. God is our Father but he is also our Mother. Isaiah 49:15 speaks of him in mothering terms; medieval devotion dwelt on the mother-love of God, and of Jesus (particularly Julian of Norwich, in chapters 57–63 of her *Revelations*); the same idea underlies the use of the pelican in Christian ikonography, for Jesus, like a mother, feeds us in the Eucharist with his own substance. Another line of imagery thinks rather of believers as the pregnant mothers in whom Christ must be formed and brought to birth (cf. Galatians 4:19). This is taken further in John 16:21–22 where Jesus, alluding to Isaiah 26:18; 66:7, compares his approaching death and resurrection to a painful birth; the apostles, who represent the new Messianic people, must undergo the labour and "sorrow" of bearing the risen Lord, who is "first-born from the dead". A similar idea underlies Revelation 12:1–6. There is obvious inconsistency between these two different lines of imagery, but perhaps there is a similar paradox in ordinary human begetting, conceiving and bearing. The parents are bringing the child to birth, but the child carries within it the seed of the parents' life and hope, their stake in the future.

7. *A Celebration of Failure*

1. So in William Horwood's beautiful novel Comfrey found his way to help in Rebecca's desolation, and in so doing grew stronger himself: "He had bullied and fooled her into coming, to show her these flowers to remind her that just as they had survived the fire, so, somehow, Bracken would survive and come back. But what made her weep was that Comfrey had thought to do it, loving her enough to think of a way to make her see again something of the joy in Duncton Wood that once, so long ago, she had so often celebrated and to make her see that she would not always stand alone . . . 'Oh, Comfrey!' she said again, going to him and nuzzling him close. As she did so, a wonderful look of strength came into Comfrey's normally nervous face, for he had never, ever in his whole life, felt quite so proud" (William Horwood, *Duncton Wood* (Feltham, Middlesex, Hamlyn Publishing Group, 1983), pp. 555–6). In all three parables of Luke 15 Jesus is trying to strike a chord in human nature itself, even in that of the scribes and Pharisees: "What man of you . . . or what woman . . . does not . . .?" The question is not explicitly asked in the parable of the Prodigal Son, but the force of this third story is that the father responds as fatherhood would, and even the most crabbed of the hearers can recognize it. The word "father" occurs eleven times in this parable. Jesus is not describing a fatherhood sublime and crazy, but something within our experience which points towards God. Nevertheless it is noteworthy that in the first two parables the onus of the action is on the shepherd and the woman, who actively seek what they have lost; in the third, climactic parable the father does not go out looking for his son. At this point the story ceases to reflect our ordinary experience, because God's way was to make the homeward journey himself in one of us, one in whom for the first time, albeit at the pig-trough, human nature "came to itself". Parables help us to understand, because they draw attention to some continuity between our human experience and the reality of God, but that reality transcends all human statements.

2. John Donne, "Holy Sonnets", V. Quoted from Helen Gardner, *op. cit.*

3. *Hysterein*, see p. 99 above.

4. From the Easter hymn *Exsultet*, trans. ICEL, Inc.

5. Theodulf of Orleans, quoted in *More Latin Lyrics, from Virgil to Milton*, translated by Helen Waddell, edited and with an Introduction by D. Felicitas Corrigan (London, Victor Gollancz Ltd, 1976), pp. 211–13.

6. Julian of Norwich, *op. cit*, chapter 51.

7. Trans. ICEL, Inc. (my italics). This prayer is now optional.

8. St Leo the Great, Sixth Sermon on Lent.

8. *"I Can't Pray"*
1. A friend who worked for a time in Saudi Arabia told me that she was at first puzzled by the daily traffic jams on roads leading from Riyadh out to the desert. Later she went out with friends to investigate. Many Arab families living in urban conditions felt the need to go into the desert to watch the sun set and say their evening prayers. They would drive out of the town for a few miles, stop at the roadside and then walk a short distance into the desert to sit and think. Most of these people were the first generation to be living in permanent houses. Everything that mattered to them culturally and spiritually came from the desert, and they found it necessary to go back there frequently.

9. *The Eastering Spirit*
1. The Fathers of the Church liked to say that as the Law had been a pedagogue or tutor for the Jews, leading them to Christ (cf. Galatians 3:24), so had philosophy been for the Greeks. It seems legitimate to draw the further parallel: science and technology should similarly be a pedagogue to Christ for our modern world, for they are part of today's "philosophy", the achievement of the rational mind, and therefore God-given. According to the vision of Teilhard de Chardin they should lead us towards Christ, the Omega-point of the entire cosmic evolution; for evolution,

having proceeded without us for millions of years, now requires our reasonable and free collaboration to attain its end. But as in the case of the Law and philosophy, science going its own way in disobedience misleads.

2. G. M. Hopkins, *op. cit.*

3. Sir Lewis Morris (1833–1907), "The Epic of Hades", Marsyas.

4. Julian of Norwich, *Revelations of Divine Love*, chapter 11.

Bible References
Unless otherwise stated biblical references are taken from the Revised Standard Version of the Bible (RSV). The other translations used are:

AV   Authorized Version (King James Version).

JB   Jerusalem Bible, published in Great Britain by Darton, Longman & Todd Ltd, and in the United States of America by Doubleday & Company, Inc., © 1966, 1967 and 1968.

NEB   New English Bible, published by the University Presses of Oxford and Cambridge, © 1961, 1970.

Acknowledgements

The author and publisher are grateful for the use of various extracts of copyright material used in this book, publication details of which have been fully credited in the Notes to the relevant chapters.

OTHER TITLES FROM ST. BEDE'S

Spirituality Recharted *Hubert van Zeller*

In this delightful book, Dom Hubert presents one of his favorite themes: "the pursuit of sanctity by responding to the grace of spirituality." The method of approach is basically that of putting into everyday language St. John of the Cross' treatment of the soul's progress toward union with God. A best-seller!
Paperback, 157 pages $4.95

By Death Parted *Philip Jebb, editor*

Six widows from England share with you the accounts of their first years of widowhood and how they learned to cope with the loneliness and problems of being "suddenly single." The book offers consolation as well as practical advice for all who have been recently widowed.
Paperback, 101 pages $5.95

Reflections *Charles Rich*

In this profound book Charles Rich will help you in your search for personal growth in holiness. Each short chapter is full of spiritual wisdom and covers such topics as the mystery of our own being, love without limits, and the nature of prayer.
Paperback, 131 pages $6.95

Victory Over Death *Ronda Chervin*

This beautiful book is meant for all of us—because no one can escape the mystery of death. Not only will it help you to overcome the fear of death, but it will also help you to deal with all aspects of death: your own or that of a loved one. A great consolation for all!
Paperback, 63 pages $3.95

Order From:

St. Bede's Publications
P.O. Box 545
Petersham, MA 01366-0545

Please allow 4 weeks for delivery
Prices subject to change without notice
Send for our complete catalog of books and tapes.